Card Tricks

PICK A CARD

Card Tricks

TOP THAT™

Licensed exclusively to Top That Publishing Ltd
Tide Mill Way, Woodbridge, Suffolk, IP12 1AP, UK
www.topthatpublishing.com
Copyright © 2014 Tide Mill Media

Tricks of the Trade

Card tricks may seem easy to perform, but not everyone can do them. To become a magnificent trickster, you need to learn the hints and top card tricks in this section.

This section is all about card tricks. First, you'll learn all of the moves you need to know – including how to cut the cards and a crafty way of shuffling the pack – to fool any audience.

Card Tricks

Before you try some of the more complicated tricks it's best to master some easy ones first. Don't move onto the harder tricks until you've got the hang of these as they will give you the confidence to confound your audience.

When you feel ready, move onto the more advanced tricks. You'll love seeing the confused faces in your audience as people try to work out how you've fooled them. Don't tell them though, you'll have more fun seeing your tricks work over and over again!

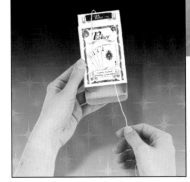

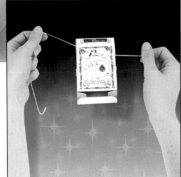

Practise, Practise, Practise

The importance of practice shouldn't be underestimated!

Make it Easy

The more you practise the more you will be able to make the most complicated tricks look effortless, and it will really boost your confidence for when it's time to perform. As you start to improve you'll be able to attempt more difficult illusions, and you can even start creating your own!

Be Confident

Practice is also important when it comes to shuffling the cards. It may take a little while to feel completely confident holding a pack of cards and shuffling them between your hands. Make sure you can do this with ease before you perform any of the tricks.

Perfect Patter

This is really important! If you draw your audience into your performance with some really slick chat, you will divert their attention from what you are doing with your hands!

Smile!

Smile at them and include lines such as 'Here's a trick that's just a little bit different …' or 'Now this trick is unbelievable …' Humour can also be used to great effect as the audience will find it more difficult to see what you are doing if they are laughing.

Double Trouble

Never perform the same trick twice in front of the same audience. You don't want them to guess your secrets!

Cutting the Cards and Shaping the Fan

Before you can become a real card magician you need to learn a few basics. Here's a good place to start.

1. Lift off around half the pack and place it to one side.

2. Take what was the bottom half and put it on top of the other pile. You have now cut the cards.

3. Now it's time to make the pack into a fan shape. Hold the pack in your left hand, making sure your thumb touches the lower end of the pack.

4. Put your right hand on the pack with your fingers at one end and your thumb at the other.

Bend the cards over your left forefinger. Move your right hand in a circular motion to the right, letting the cards fan out from your fingers.

5. When all of the cards are spread, you have completed the fan shape.

Crafty Cut

Make it look as if you have cut the cards when really you haven't changed the order at all!

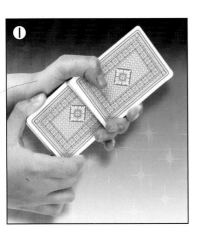

1. Hold the pack in your left hand and take about half the cards off from the bottom with your right hand.

2. Bring the bottom cards towards your body. Now take them over the cards in your left hand and place them down on the table.

3. Take the top half of the pack in your right hand, moving your right hand slightly upwards.

4. Place the cards on top of the ones on the table.

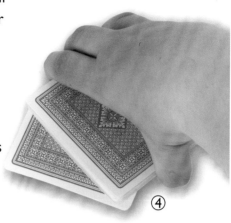

Pick a Card
Force someone to choose the card you want them to without them realising!

1. Shuffle the pack, but while you are shuffling, angle the cards so you can sneak a peek at the bottom card. Complete the shuffle, making sure you remember the bottom card.

2. Hold the pack behind your back and turn around so you are facing away from your audience. Ask a volunteer to take some cards from the top of the pack. When this is done turn around. As you do this, secretly move the card you remembered from the bottom of the pack to the top.

3. Tell your volunteer that enough cards have been taken. Then say, 'Will you take the next card please?'

4. Then, ask them to hand the card back to you. Taking care not to look at it, hold the card up to your volunteer so that they can see the face.

5. If the card you remembered was, for example, the ace of hearts, ask your volunteer if that is their card. They will be amazed that you are right!

Overhand Shuffle

All card players use this simple shuffling technique.

1. Hold the cards in your left hand, as in the picture.

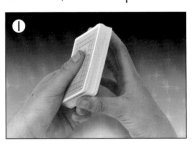

2. Take most of the bottom half of the cards with your right hand and lift them over the cards in your left hand.

3. Put your left thumb on the back of the cards in your right hand and take some cards off the top of the ones in your left hand.

4. Keep repeating this action until all the cards are in your left hand.

Shuffle Management

Your chosen card will be on top of the pack, even after shuffling!

1. Shuffle the cards and spread them out into a fan. Ask a volunteer to take a card and remember it. Now ask them to put it back, this time on top of the pack.

2. When the chosen card is put back on the pack, give the pack an overhand shuffle. When you shuffle make sure you don't lose track of the chosen card. Do this by simply making sure it goes from the top of the pack to the bottom.

3. Do another overhand shuffle, but this time keep going until you have only the chosen card in your right hand. Then simply drop it back on top of the pack.

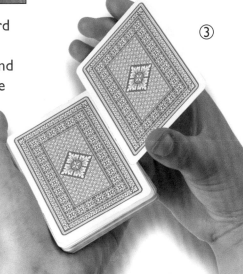

Feel the Force

This is another way of forcing someone to take the card of your choice.

1. The card that you will force someone to choose is at the bottom of the pack, so before you begin the trick, take a secret look at that card and remember it.

2. Tell a volunteer from your audience that you will force them to choose a card and name the card from the bottom of the pack. Hold the cards in your left hand, and place your right hand on top of them, with your right thumb underneath.

3. With the fingers of your right hand, move the cards back a few at a time. Ask your volunteer to say 'stop' at any time while you are doing this.

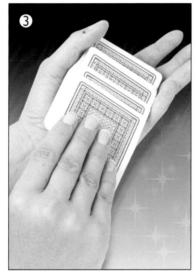

4. Pull back all the cards you have moved with your right hand. At the same time, drag the bottom card

with your right thumb so that it is underneath the cards in your right hand. Hold up these cards to show the bottom one – it is, of course, the card which you told your audience you would find in step 2.

Spread

You will often need to display all the cards. One way is to spread the cards out evenly on a table.

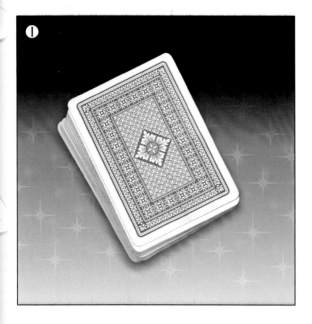

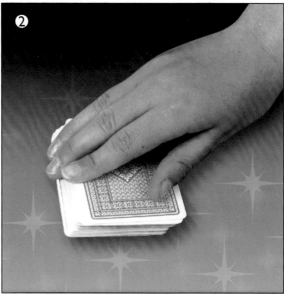

1. Lay the pack on the table.

2. Lay your right hand flat on top of the pack, making sure your fingers extend beyond the edge of the cards.

3. Push down lightly and move your hand to the right. The cards will spread out from the bottom, moved by your fingertips.

Trickery Tip

This may take some practice but when you get it right, your routine will seem really sharp!

One Good Turn

You'll look very cool with this neat move!

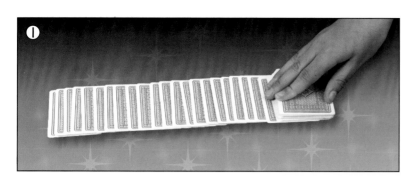

1. Lay the cards face down on a flat surface. Make sure you spread them out evenly. If they are not even, the trick will not work very well.

2. Put your left forefinger under the card furthest to the left.

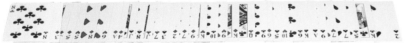

3. Lift the side of the card up and then push it over so it is face up. This will make all the other cards turn over as well.

Trickery Tip

Practise your tricks on your own first, then you will really impress your audience when you perform them for real!

Bungling Burglars

You will need a deck of cards to tell the tale of the four bungling burglars who are caught making their getaway!

Pack of cards

1. Show the four Jacks in a fan shape (as in the picture on the left), but don't let your audience see that there are three other cards (any cards) hidden in front of the first Jack. Tuck them away tightly.

2. Close the fan and put it on top of the deck, explaining that the Jacks are burglars and the deck is the building.

3. Tell your tale of the burglars roaming the building to do their wicked business. Each burglar is moved to a different floor by removing the top card each time and placing it elsewhere in the pack as you talk. Move the top card to the 'lower floors' and the next two burglars to 'higher floors'. Put the fourth burglar on the bottom as a lookout.

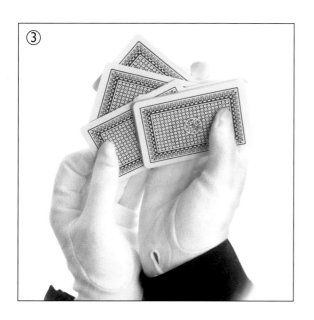

③

4. Remove this bottom 'lookout' and say he has spotted the police coming. He rushes to the top of the building (place him on top of the pack) and calls to his gang.

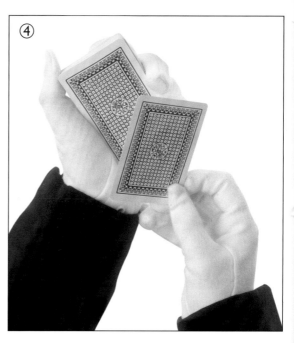

④

5. Deal the top four cards and explain that they are all making their getaway.

6. Turn over the four cards you have dealt. Surprise surprise, they are the four Jacks!

⑥

Tricky Turnover

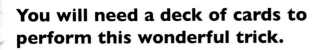

You will need a deck of cards to perform this wonderful trick.

1. Hold the cards face down and secretly turn over the bottom card. Spread them out and ask a member of your audience to pick one. Make sure the bottom, face-up card doesn't show.

Props box

• Pack of cards

2. Ask your volunteer to show the chosen card to everyone. While all eyes are on this, turn the pack over in your hands. Let them replace the card, face down, anywhere in the deck.

②

③

3. Now say you will use your magic powers to turn the chosen card over, even though you don't know which one it is. Hold the deck behind your back and turn the reversed card face up.

4. Spread out all the cards, face up. Somewhere in the middle of the cards will be a card that is face down – the very card that was chosen!

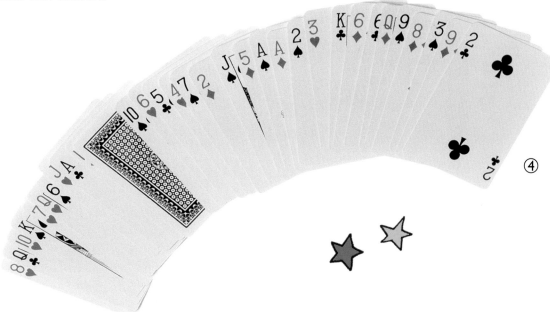

④

Magic Facts

Many TV magicians perform in front of a live audience to provide the television viewing public with some reassurance that the illusions are not visual effects set up by the production and crew.

This is your Card

Convince your audience that you can find a chosen card, just by checking someone's pulse as they pass their hand over the pack!

Props box

• Pack of cards

①

1. Ask someone in your audience to shuffle the cards. Turn the cards face down and spread them out in a fan shape. Now ask someone to take out any card and remember it.

2. Allow them to show the card to everybody else. While this is being done, secretly look at the bottom of the deck. You must remember this card. Then ask for the chosen card to be replaced on the top of the deck.

②

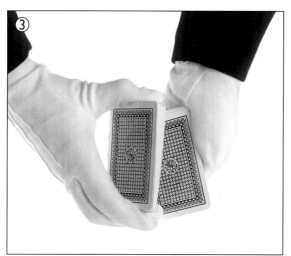
③

4. Take the wrist of the person who chose the card, and find their pulse with your finger. Guide their hand slowly over all the cards on the table, explaining that you will feel their pulse quicken when it passes over their card.

④

3. Now cut the pack somewhere in the middle, and put the bottom half of the pack on top. The chosen card is now halfway down the pack. Give the deck a few more cuts to make sure the chosen card really is lost in the deck. Spread the cards face up across a table top.

5. When you find the chosen card, push their hand down to point to it. The secret of this trick is that the card on the right of the one you have remembered (from the bottom of the deck) is the chosen card!

⑤

Clipped

This trick is so simple, it's a nice easy card trick to start with. Use an old pack of cards and practise your performance skills!

Preparation

Prepare the trick by gluing the cards in a neat row with the Queen in the middle of the Aces, as shown.

Props box

- A paper clip
- Four Aces and any Queen from an old pack of cards
- Glue

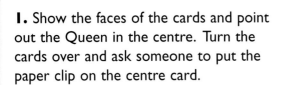

2. When you turn the cards back, the clip is strangely nowhere near the centre card!

1. Show the faces of the cards and point out the Queen in the centre. Turn the cards over and ask someone to put the paper clip on the centre card.

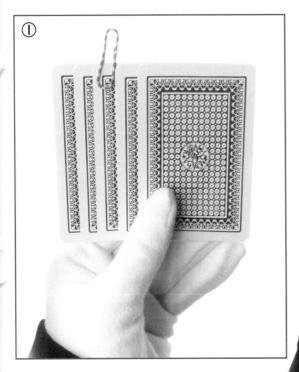

Vanishing Ace

Make an Ace disappear and then reappear somewhere else, by magic! How did you do that?

Preparation

Secretly hide the Ace of Diamonds somewhere in the room.

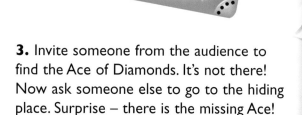

Props box

• Pack of cards

①

3. Invite someone from the audience to find the Ace of Diamonds. It's not there! Now ask someone else to go to the hiding place. Surprise – there is the missing Ace!

1. Show the other Aces to your audience, holding them so that only the tip of the Ace of Hearts is showing. Tell your audience that you are holding the Ace of Clubs, the Ace of Diamonds, and the Ace of Spades, and that you are going to make the Ace of Diamonds disappear.

2. Turn the cards over and return them to the deck in different places. Shuffle the cards yourself, or pass them to a volunteer to shuffle.

③

Finger Shuffle

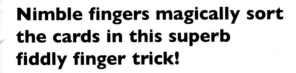

Nimble fingers magically sort the cards in this superb fiddly finger trick!

Props box

• Pack of cards

1. Ask someone to hold out their hands with their fingers touching the tabletop, just as if they were playing the piano.

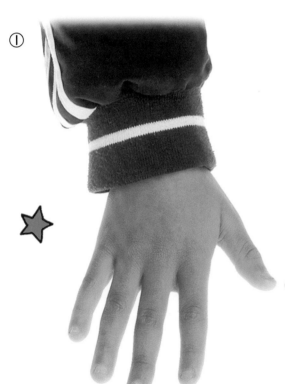

2. Take pairs of cards from the deck and place them between the fingers of each hand, calling out 'even' each time. Do this with all the spaces between the fingers, except one. Into this last space put one card and say 'odd'. Put aside the rest of the cards.

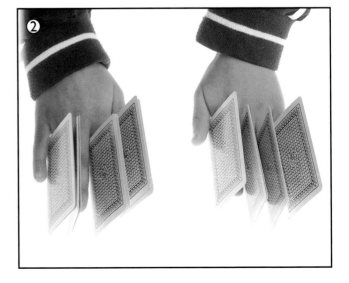

③

3. Take each pair of cards from between the fingers and lay them side by side on the table, making two piles, and saying 'even' each time you do so.

4. Now take the single card. Let your volunteer choose which pile to place it on. Tap both piles and say you will now make the 'odd' card jump from one pile to the other.

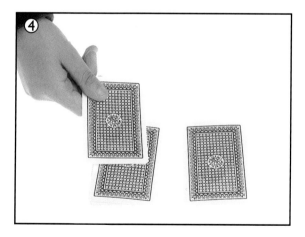

④

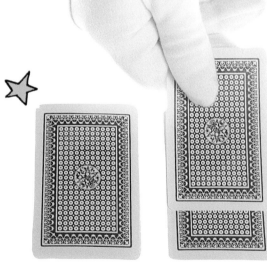

⑤

5. Deal out the cards from the chosen pile in pairs, saying 'even' each time. Amazingly, it is now even. Do the same with the other pile, dealing out pairs, and you will be left with one 'odd' card, just as you promised!

Trickery Tip

Involve your audience as much as you can in the performance to make them feel part of it.

Pick a Card

This classic trick fools people time after time! See if you can keep up a constant stream of patter whilst you do it!

Props box

• Pack of cards

①

1. Offer your pack of cards to a member of your audience. Ask for the cards to be shuffled. Take them back and fan them out. Ask for a brave volunteer to pick any card.

2. Ask the volunteer to look at their card, remember which it is, but not tell you. Then cut the pack and ask them to replace their card, remembering which card it was. It doesn't matter where they put it back in the pack.

②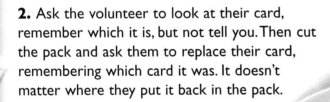

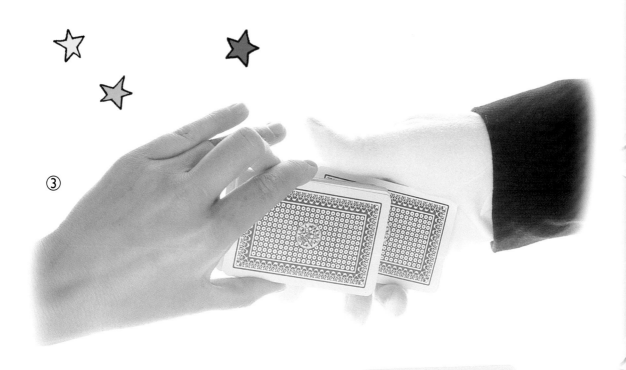

③

④

3. Cut the pack of cards one or two times so the chosen card is completely lost. Tap the card and say 'Abracadabra!' very dramatically.

4. Turn the cards over and find the chosen card. Hold it up so that your volunteer can confirm it is the card that they picked! Wow, amazing!

Trickery Tip

One simple, secret move makes this trick work. As your volunteer looks at their chosen card, secretly tip the cards in your top hand until you can see above the cut. When the card is replaced you will know which card it is next to. When the cards are face up, the chosen card will be on the right of the card you remembered.

Magic Shuffle

Magically deal a line of cards in perfect order! You'll baffle your audience with your outstanding trickery!

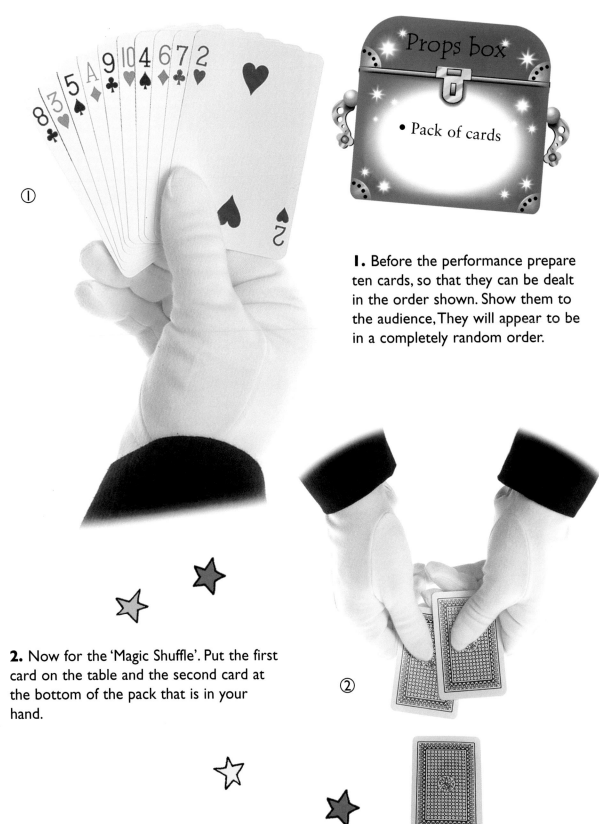

①

Props box

• Pack of cards

1. Before the performance prepare ten cards, so that they can be dealt in the order shown. Show them to the audience, They will appear to be in a completely random order.

2. Now for the 'Magic Shuffle'. Put the first card on the table and the second card at the bottom of the pack that is in your hand.

②

③

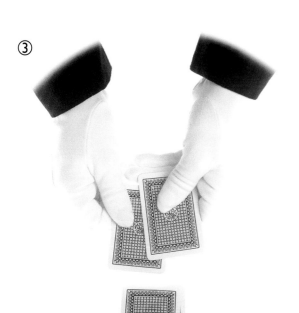

3. Put the third card on top of the one on the table and the fourth at the bottom of the deck. Continue until all the cards are on the table.

4. Pick up the pack and glance through it with dismay. The trick hasn't worked! You forgot to say the magic words, 'Magic Shuffle!'

④

⑤

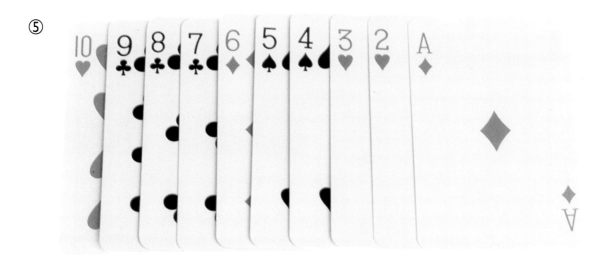

5. Perform the same shuffle again, but this time saying the magic words ('Magic Shuffle!'). When you deal the cards this time, face up in a line on the table; they will be in perfect order! That's the Magic Shuffle!

Trickery Tip

Preparation and practice are vital for the success of this trick. Make sure you know exactly what to do before you start a performance.

Telepathy Test

Demonstrate your baffling powers with this fantastic telepathy test!

1. Shuffle a deck of cards and lay nine cards face up on the table in three rows of three.

Props box

• Pack of cards
• A secret accomplice

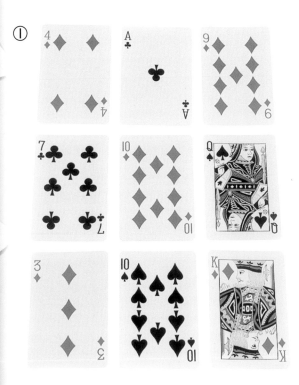

2. Give the rest of the pack to a 'volunteer'. Explain you will leave the room for a few moments so the audience can choose one of the cards on the table.

3. Return to the room. Make a play of concentrating, then announce the number chosen. Amazing!

But How?

Your volunteer must be your secret assistant. Imagine the deck of cards divided into a grid, matching the one on the table. The assistant just needs to hold the deck with their thumb on the imaginary square indicating the card chosen.

Quick Change

How can a card be both red and black? Let's find out in this great trick!

Props box

- Two spare cards
- A joker

Preparation

You need to make a special card for this trick, using two cards, plus the Joker. To make the special card, fold the two spare cards exactly in half. Glue the bottom halves back to back. Glue the Joker behind the other halves with the patterned back outwards.

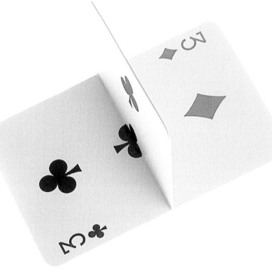

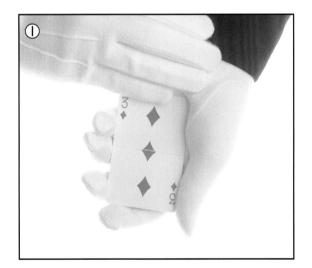

1. Hold the card up to your audience with the Three of Diamonds visible. Cover it with your hand, then slide your hand downwards and reveal the Three of Clubs.

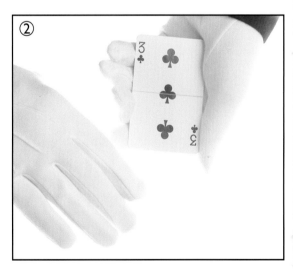

2. Repeat the movement, this time sliding your hand upwards to reveal the original Three of Diamonds. Practise the action in front of a mirror until you're happy it looks convincing.

Abracadabra

A magic spell locates a chosen card! This trick requires excellent sleight-of-hand and a calm nerve.

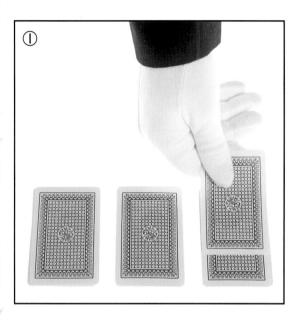

1. Deal three piles of cards, face down, until you have seven in each pile. Set aside the rest of the deck.

2. Ask someone to pick one of the piles.

3. Display the chosen cards in a fan to your volunteer. Ask your volunteer to choose a card, but not tell you what it is.

Magic Facts

Many magicians have assistants who help the main magician in a number of ways, including holding props, assisting in acts and sometimes misdirecting the audience's attention.

4. Gather up the cards and put the pile containing the chosen card in between the other two piles. Deal the cards in the same way again into three piles of seven.

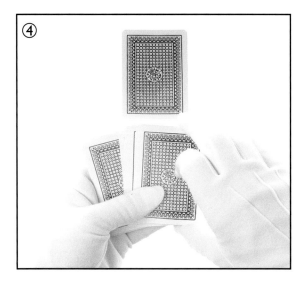

5. Pick up one pile at a time and display them to the volunteer, asking them to identify the pile which contains their chosen card.

6. Once again, put this pile between the other two and deal out the cards into three piles.

7. Fan out the cards for a third time: ask the volunteer to identify the pile containing their card, then put this pile between the other two.

8. Solemnly spell out the word ABRACADABRA, dealing one card for each of the letters intoned. Turn over the final card to show it is the chosen one!

But How?

This trick only works if you deal three piles at a time, instead of dealing one pile of seven followed by another two piles of seven.

Magnetic Attraction

Two cards, chosen at random, come together in the pack.

1. Have the cards shuffled and cut into two piles. You take one pile and a volunteer takes the other.

2. Ask the volunteer to look through the cards in their half of the pack, take one out, remember it, place it on the top of the pile, and then put the pile on the table.

3. You appear to do exactly the same, but what you really do is look at and remember the card on the bottom of your pile. You take no notice whatsoever of the card you took from the pack.

28

4. Put your pile of cards on top of the volunteer's and then ask for the pack to be cut several times.

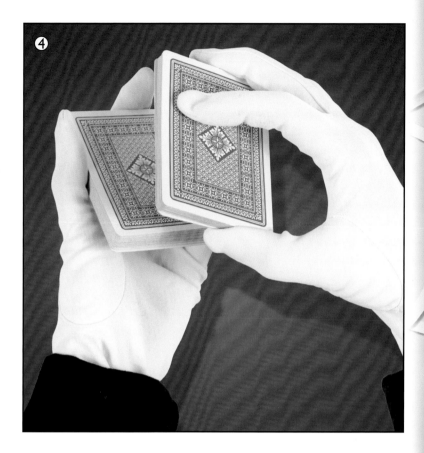

5. Now say that you will cause the two cards to come together in the pack. Ask the volunteer for the name of his or her chosen card.

6. You name the card you saw on the bottom of the pack as your chosen card.

7. When the volunteer looks through the pack, the two 'chosen' cards will be together.

Royal Traveller

The King of Hearts from your hand seems to disappear and reappear at the other side of the room.

Props box
- Pack of cards
- Spare King of Hearts
- Ace of Spades
- Scissors and glue

1. Prepare your trick by gluing a King of Hearts at an angle onto the face of an Ace of Spades. Then cut the excess from the edges of the King of Hearts.

2. Hide your spare King of Hearts in the room, behind an ornament or on a bookshelf, to retrieve at the end of the trick.

3. Hold two other Aces together and place them on top of the King, so it looks as if you are holding two Aces with a King in between. Show the fan of cards to your audience, face up.

4. Now turn the fan over, and at the same time spread the cards to separate the two Aces. Ask someone to take out the King.

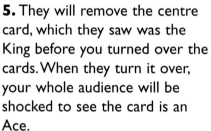

④

Trickery Tip

Using props, such as a magic wand or a handkerchief, helps to distract your audience from the trick.

5. They will remove the centre card, which they saw was the King before you turned over the cards. When they turn it over, your whole audience will be shocked to see the card is an Ace.

⑤

6. Now direct someone to the real King in its hiding place. That's amazing!

⑥

Runaway Couple

Find a pair of cards hidden in the deck!

Preparation

Before doing this trick, put the Seven of Hearts on the bottom of the deck and the Eight of Diamonds on the top. Return the deck to its box.

Props box

• Pack of cards

①

1. Hold up the deck, look through it and take out the Seven of Diamonds and Eight of Hearts. Hold them up quickly to your audience and say, 'I am now going to put these into the centre of the deck ... and then I shall use my amazing powers to find them again.'

2. Hold the deck between finger and thumb. Give a quick flip so that the cards fly out of your hand, but keep hold of the top and bottom cards.

③

②

3. Show the two cards left in your hand and take a bow. As long as you did not draw attention to the face values, the audience will not notice that the cards have changed.

32

Window of the Mind

Every time the cards are shuffled and returned to their pack, you can name the bottom card!

Props box
• Pack of cards

1. Ask a member of your audience to shuffle the cards and remember the bottom one.

2. Hold out the case for them to return the pack.

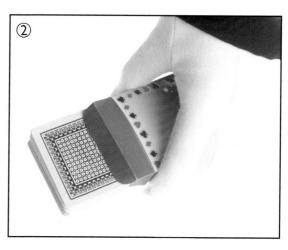

3. Without having seen the card, you can name it for them! This is easy, because you have already prepared the case by cutting a small window in the bottom corner. You can even repeat this trick with another member of your audience. Just be careful that you hold out the case with your hand covering the window.

TA-DAH!!

Surprise Fours

Find a chosen card – and four surprises!

1. Before you start, turn over a Five and put it on top of the pack. On top of that, put all the Fours, face down. Ask a member of your audience to choose a card. Put it on the bottom of the pack.

2. Cut the pack, so the chosen card is now next to the top Four.

3. Spread out the cards until you come to the reversed Five.

Props box

• Pack of cards

4. Count five cards along and push out the chosen card. Take away all the cards to the right of the chosen card and to the left of the Five, so you are left with six cards on the table.

5. Reveal the chosen card for the audience to see, and stop as if the trick is finished. Then say, 'But here is something more amazing!' – and turn over all the fours!

Fan-Tastic

Amaze your audience with your magic 'sticky' cards.

Preparation

Cut out a large circle from the back of a spare card. Fold the circle in half and glue one half in the middle on the back of the Jack of Diamonds. The unglued half should stand upright, but be disguised by the pattern.

Props box

- Pack of cards
- A spare playing card

1. Practise handling your new card; you need to be able to flatten the tab on the back so that it looks like an ordinary playing card when it is mixed in with the other cards. For the trick, you should lay the card on your palm, face up, with the secret tab tucked between two fingers.

2. Place several other cards between the trick card and your fingers. Slot them randomly around the first card. Then turn your hand over and the cards will appear to be magically stuck to your hand!

3. To finish the trick, simply let go of the tab, allowing the cards to fall onto the table. As you gather them up, flatten the tab so it is hidden again.

The Chosen Card

A card chosen by a member of your audience is lost in the deck, but you can still find it.

Props box

• Pack of cards
• A table

①

1. Ask a member of your audience to shuffle a deck of cards. Now take the deck and ask them to select a card and show it to the rest of the audience.

2. While they are doing this, quickly and secretly look at the card that is on the bottom of the deck.

②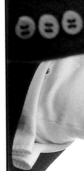

③

3. Now divide the deck into two. Put the top half of the cards into your left hand. Ask your volunteer to place the chosen card on top of the bottom half. Then put the remainder of the cards on top of it.

④

4. The chosen card will now be below the card you looked at. To make your trick even more convincing, cut the cards again.

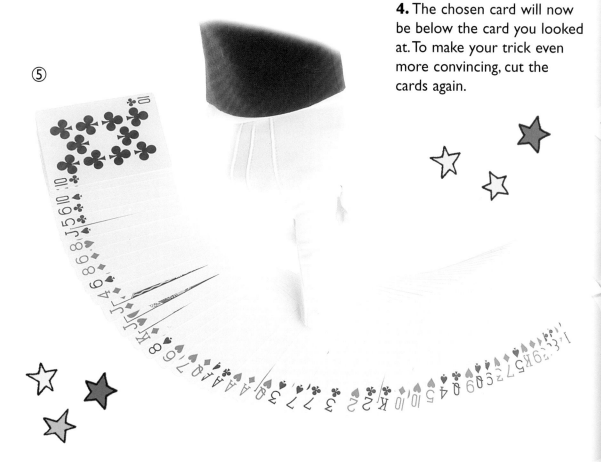
⑤

5. Spread the deck of cards face up on the table. The card chosen by your volunteer will be on top of the card that was on the bottom of the deck in step 2.

Magic Facts

Siegfried and Roy were two illusionists and entertainers who were very well-known for using white tigers and lions in their shows. They performed at The Mirage in Las Vegas for over 10 years.

Feel the Force

You force someone to choose the card that you want them to.

Preparation

The card which you will force someone to choose is at the bottom of the deck, so before you begin the trick, take a secret look at that card and remember it.

1. Tell a volunteer from your audience that you will force them to choose a card – name the card from the bottom of the deck. Hold the place cards in your left hand, and place your right hand on top of them, with your right thumb underneath.

2. With the fingers of your right hand, move the cards back a few at a time. Ask your volunteer to say 'stop' at any time while you are doing this.

3. Pull back all the cards you have moved with your right hand. At the same time, drag the bottom card with your right thumb so that it is underneath the cards in your right hand. Hold up these cards to show the bottom one – it is, of course, the card which you told your audience you would find.

52 Card Pick-Up

This is a spectacular way to find a chosen card – but it takes nerve!

1. Start by losing, and then finding a chosen card (see pages 36-37). Cut the card into the top of the deck, as shown.

①

2. Now ask your volunteer to hold their hand out, palm up. Then position the deck face up in their hand, so their fingers stretch underneath the cards for at least 4 cm (1.5 in.) and their thumb is on the top of the deck about 2.5 cm (1 in.). Ask them to hold the deck firmly.

②

③

④

3. Get ready! With your hand, strike down on the end of the deck that is not being held.

4. All the cards will scatter onto the table, except the chosen card, which is being held firmly between the fingers and thumb of your volunteer.

Mega Mind Reading

What is better than reading one person's mind? Reading two, of course!

Props box

- Pack of cards
- A pencil

Preparation

Prepare your trick. Take any card, and on its back put one pencil dot in the top left hand and bottom right hand corners. Put this card in your pocket until you are ready to use it.

1. Shuffle the deck of cards, then ask two volunteers to select a card each, which they need to remember without telling anyone.

2. While they are remembering their cards, secretly retrieve the marked card from your pocket and put it on the bottom of the deck.

3. Ask one of your volunteers to replace their card on top of the deck. Cut the deck. Place the top half of the cards in your left hand, then put the other half on top. The marked card is now on top of the first chosen card.

4. Spread the deck face down to find your marked card. Cut the deck in half, one card below the marked card. Then put the top half of cards underneath. This takes the first chosen card to the bottom of the deck, with the marked card above it. Quickly look at the bottom card, and remember it.

5. Ask your second volunteer to place their card on the top of the deck. Cut the deck, as you did in step 3, to bring the first and second chosen cards, and the marked card together.

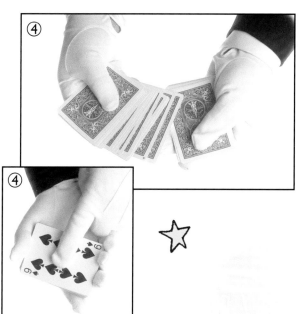

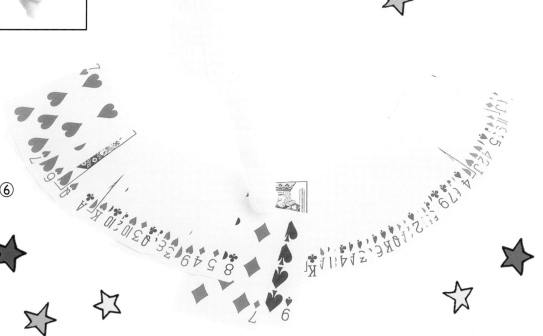

6. Announce to your audience that you will now read your first volunteer's mind! Make a big show of concentrating hard, closing your eyes, and breathing deeply. Then reveal the name of the chosen card (which you found out in step 4) ask your volunteer to confirm that this is the right one, and your audience will gasp!

7. They will be even more amazed when you complete the trick, and read your second volunteer's mind. To do this, spread the pack of cards in front of you. The second chosen card will be on top of the first chosen card. Of course, now that you know the secret of how to read two minds at once, there's no reason why you can't read three, four, or even five!

Back-to-Back

You show your audience two cards and hold them face-to-face. When you blow on them, they are suddenly back-to-back!

1. Hold a card in each hand by its side between your thumb and first finger – the faces should be opposite each other. Now position your hands about 30 cm (12 in.) apart.

Props box

• One pair of cards the same number and the same colour

3. Raise the cards towards your mouth and tell your audience that you will blow between them, and they will magically change places.

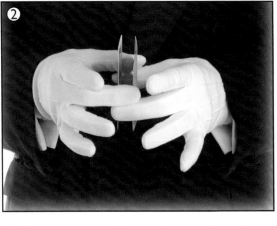

2. Bring your hands together until each card can be gripped by the thumb and second finger of the opposite hand. There should be a gap of about 1 cm (¹/2 in.) between the cards.

③

4. As soon as you have blown between the cards, start to move your hands back to their original positions 30 cm (12 in.) apart, the right hand taking the left card, the left hand taking the right card.

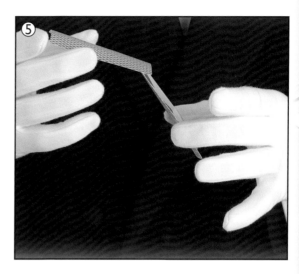

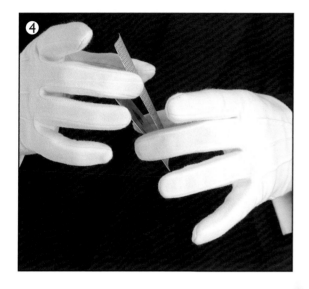

5. This trick needs a lot of practice before you perform it. Start slowly and gradually build up speed until you can make the exchange without hesitation. It is the smoothness of your move which will fool your audience.

It's magic – the cards are now back-to-back!

TA·DAH!!

Five-Way Split

This trick uses a more complicated method to find a chosen card.

Preparation

Preparation is key to the success of this trick. Before your show, take ten diamond cards from your deck. Count out a pile of thirty-five cards – put five diamonds underneath the pile and five on top.

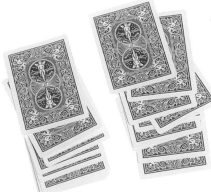

①

1. Give the deck of cards to a member of the audience, and ask them to deal the cards into five piles, face down on the table. Ask them to pick a card from the middle of the piles. They need to remember it and can show it to the audience, but you must not see what it is.

2. Tell your volunteer to put the card face down on top of any of the piles, then ask them to put the piles together and make one deck of cards. Cut the pack several times to make sure their card is well mixed in with the others.

3. Spread the deck of cards. To find the right card, scan slowly over the cards. The chosen card will be between two diamonds, so as soon as you see a card splitting two diamonds, you know you have found the right one.

Magic Touch

Here is a really impressive way of naming cards just by touching them.

Preparation

Before your show, take one card from your deck and put it in your back pocket. Remember what was on the card.

Props box

• Pack of Cards

I. Ask a member of your audience to shuffle the deck of cards for you. Take the deck, face down, behind your back, and put the hidden card face up on top. While you are doing this, pretend to the audience that you are reading the card by touch.

2. Bring the deck out from behind your back, holding it in front of you so that your audience can see the face of the card you placed on top of the deck. Name the card for the audience.

3. While you are doing this, look at the card in front of you, which is actually on the bottom of the deck, and remember it.

4. Take the deck behind your back again. Remove the card from the bottom of the deck, and place it face up on top of the card which you have just named, all the time telling your audience that you are guessing which card it is by touch alone.

5. You can now bring the cards forward and name the next card. At the same time, remember the new card on the bottom of the deck, so that you can perform the trick all over again!

The Magnificent 7

**Your prediction comes true
– your volunteer really
does choose the seven pile!**

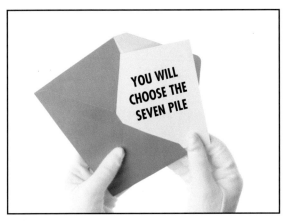

Props box

- Pack of cards
- Pen and paper
- Envelope

Preparation

Before your audience arrives, write 'You will choose the seven pile' on your paper and seal it in the envelope.

1. For your audience, deal three piles of cards, face down. What they don't know is that the piles have been arranged beforehand: the first is the four Sevens, the second is a Four, a Two and an Ace (adding up to seven), and the last pile contains any seven cards.

①

②

TA-DAH!!

2. Now ask a volunteer to choose any pile and turn it over. When the envelope is opened, your prediction is correct!

Rope Tricks

LOOP THE LOOP

Rope Tricks

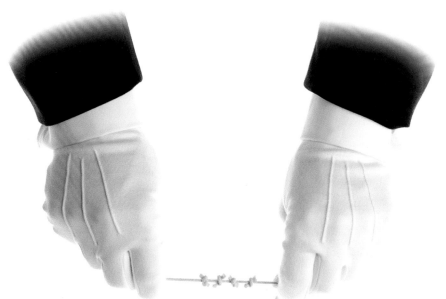

Licensed exclusively to Top That Publishing Ltd
Tide Mill Way, Woodbridge, Suffolk, IP12 1AP, UK
www.topthatpublishing.com
Copyright © 2014 Tide Mill Media
All rights reserved
0 2 4 6 8 9 7 5 3 1
Printed and bound in China

Cut Above the Rest

How can you cut a piece of string in two but leave it in one piece? Follow this trick to find out! That's magic!

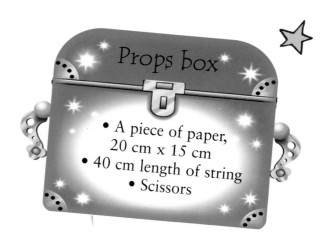

1. Fold a piece of paper as you see in the picture below. Lay the string across the paper so your audience can see it.

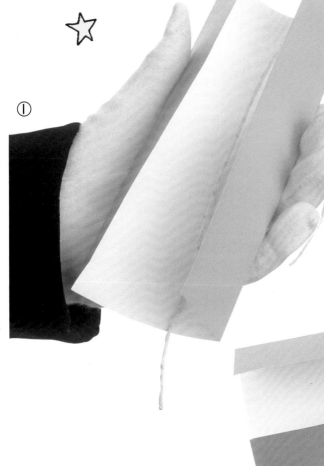

①

②

2. Now lift the paper and tip the string under the bottom fold. What your audience cannot see is that your thumb stops the centre of the string from falling down.

3. Carefully cut right through the paper from bottom to top, making sure that the scissors go behind the central part of the string (the part held back by your thumb).

③

4. Keep the two halves together so everyone thinks the string has been cut into two. Now crumple up the paper and say you will restore the string to one piece.

④

5. Pull the string out of the paper in one complete piece!

⑤

Vanishing Knots

Three knots tied around a tube vanish without any trace at all! How can this be? Spooky!

Props box

- A piece of paper 20 cm x 15 cm
- Two paper clips
- 1 m length of rope

1. Make a tube with the paper by rolling it up, then hold it in place with a paper clip at each end.

①

2. Tie three single knots around the tube with your piece of rope.

②

③

3. Push one end of the rope into the tube, followed by each of the three knots in turn. This is where the magic happens, as the knots untie themselves as they go into the tube – mask the end of the tube with your hand, or the audience will see how the trick works!

4. Keep up a patter of jokes as you come to the end of the trick to distract the audience. Now astound your audience by pulling the rope from the other end of the tube until it has all come through. They will be amazed to see that the three knots have disappeared!

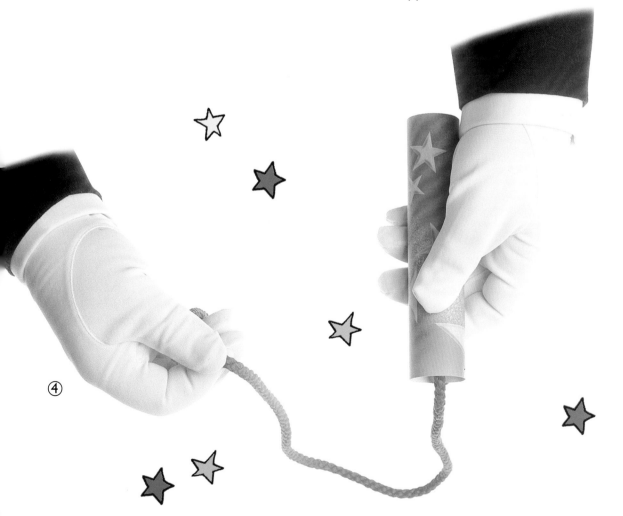

④

Loop the Loop

It looks like all you are doing is looping rope around your hand, but you are actually tying secret knots!

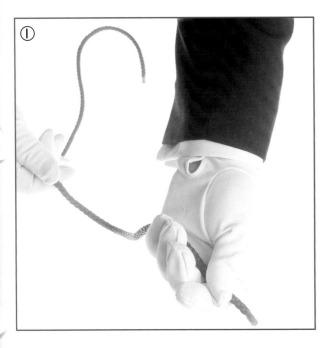

Props box

• 1 m length of string or rope

1. Hold one end of the rope firmly in your left hand, as shown left.

2. Now ask a member of the audience for a number between one and five. Using your right hand, make the same number of loops over your left fingers. It is really important that the loops you make are reverse loops, as shown.

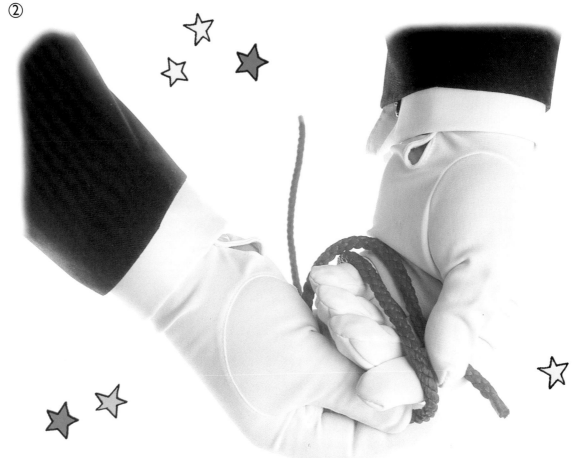

3. When you have made the right number of loops, tuck the end of the rope in your right hand through the top loop, then reach through and grip the end of the rope that you are holding in your left hand. Pull this end slowly through the loops. Remember to keep up a running patter of jokes, to keep the audience amused.

③

4. Shake the loops off your fingers, then pull gently on both ends of the rope. Amazingly, the same number of knots as the number chosen by your volunteer will form in the rope! That's just 'knot' possible!

④

Magic Facts

The world's largest magic organisation is the International Brotherhood of Magicians. With approximately 15,000 members around the globe, it publishes a monthly journal called The Linking Ring.

Many magic organisations are very secretive and require members to commit to the 'Magician's Oath', which promises never to reveal the secrets of magic to non-magicians. Once members have sworn to the oath, they are considered to be a magician.

Magic is thought to date as far back as the ancient Egyptians. Hieroglyphics (a picture of an object representing a word, syllable or sound), which were used as the ancient Egyptian alphabet, were found in an Egyptian tomb, thought to be depicting the common cup and ball trick. However, this is disputed by many and is believed by experts to actually be bakers making bread.

The Continuous Knot

You tie a knot without letting go of the ends of the rope. But, how do you do it?

Props box

- Length of string or rope

1. Hold one end of the rope in each hand, then put your right hand in front of your left hand and drape the rope over your left arm.

2. Bring your right hand in front of the loop. The loop over your arm will appear to have two sections. Your right hand now goes in through the first section, around the back of the central piece of rope, then back out to the front through the second section.

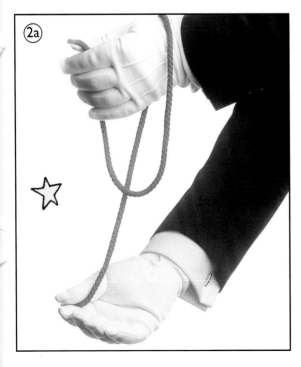

3. Move your hands apart very slowly until the loops gently tighten around your wrists.

③

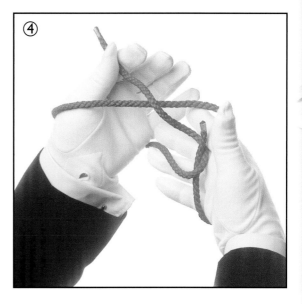

④

4. Turn your right hand inward and secretly let go of the end of the rope. Let the end fall to the other side of the loop, then quickly grab it again.

⑤

5. Shake the loops off and, still holding the two ends, pull the rope out so that a knot forms in the middle. Magic!

Magic Facts

One of the first modern day theatrical magicians was Frenchman Jean Eugène Robert-Houdin (1805–1871). He opened a magic theatre in Paris in the 1840s, and is named by many as the 'father of modern magic'.

Thumbs Up

A ring is trapped on a loop of string which is being held by a volunteer, but you still manage to release it – how?

Props box
• A ring
• A long piece of string tied into a loop

1. Borrow a ring from someone in your audience, then thread it onto the loop of string.

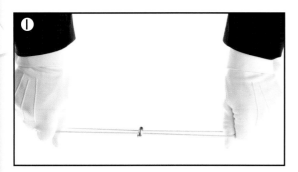

2. Ask a volunteer to hold up their thumbs, and loop the string over them so that the ring is trapped in the middle.

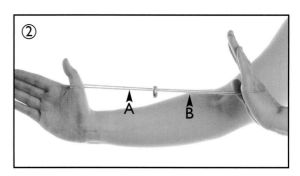

3. With your left thumb and forefinger, hold the string near your volunteer's right thumb.

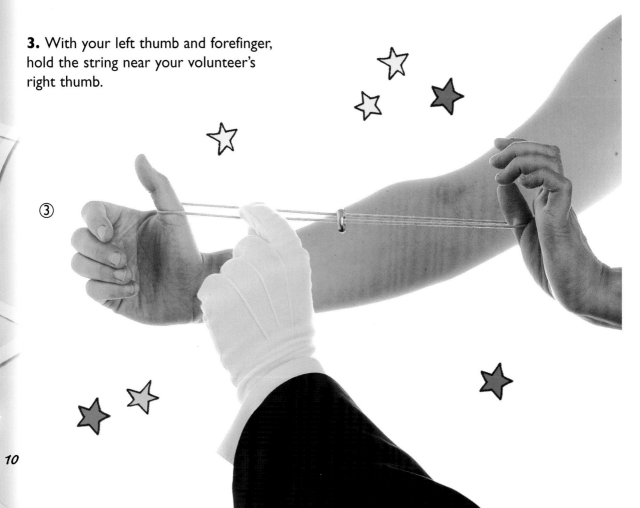

4. Using your right hand, take the string nearest to you at point A (see step 2 picture) and loop it over your volunteer's right thumb from the front.

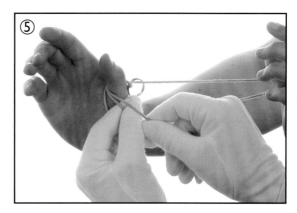

5. Push the ring as far as it will go to the left, then take the string at point B and loop it over your volunteer's right thumb again, this time from the back.

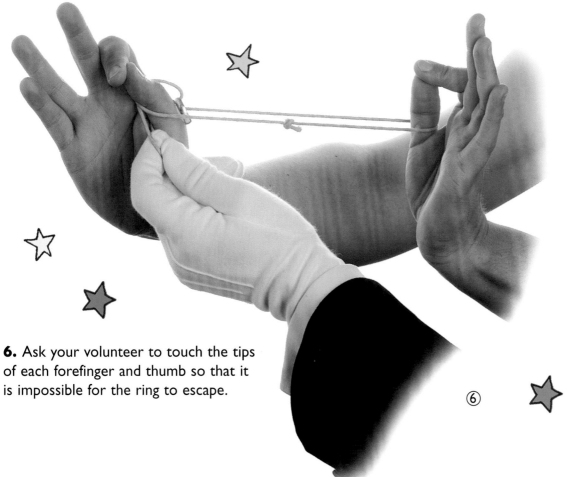

6. Ask your volunteer to touch the tips of each forefinger and thumb so that it is impossible for the ring to escape.

7. Now take hold of the ring with your right hand and let go of the string you are holding between your left thumb and forefinger.

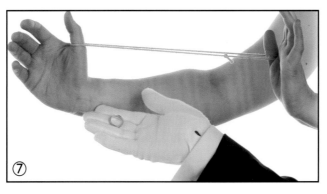

The ring jumps free of the string loop – which your volunteer is still holding!

Ring Off

You remove a ring which has been threaded onto a piece of string, even though the ends of the string are being held by two volunteers!

Preparation

Before your show, hide one of the rings underneath the handkerchief on your table.

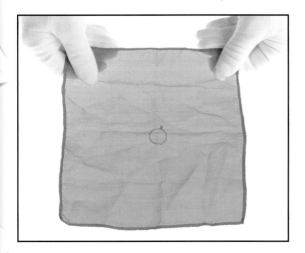

1. Start your trick by showing the second ring to your audience, then thread it onto the string.

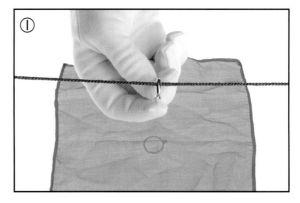

2. Lift the handkerchief and the hidden ring from your table and place both over the threaded ring.

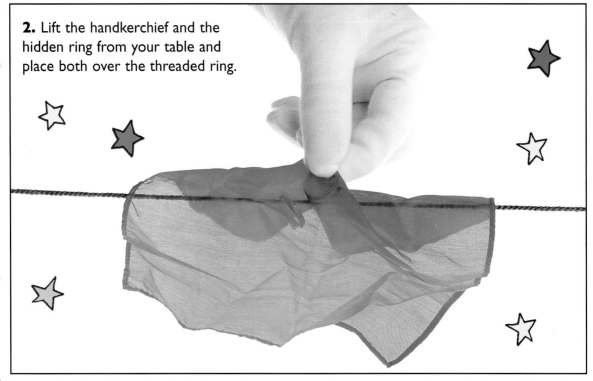

12

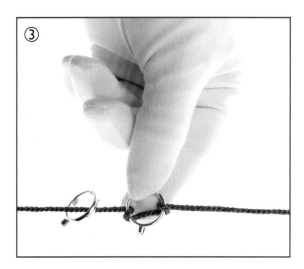
③

3. With your hands underneath the handkerchief, make the hidden ring seem looped onto the string to the left of the other ring. Simply push the string up through the ring, then loop it over the top.

4. Hold the hidden ring through the handkerchief with your left hand, while your right hand, which is still under the handkerchief, covers the other ring and slides it to the right. Ask your volunteer to hold the handkerchief and ring at the end of the string. Take hold of their end of the string and secretly move the ring into your hand.

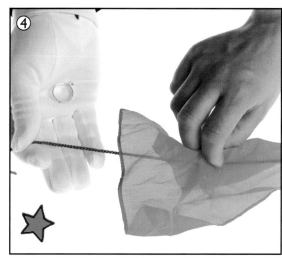
④

5. Give the end of the string back to your volunteer and hold the ring again through the handkerchief.

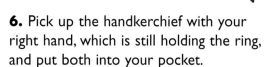

6. Pick up the handkerchief with your right hand, which is still holding the ring, and put both into your pocket.

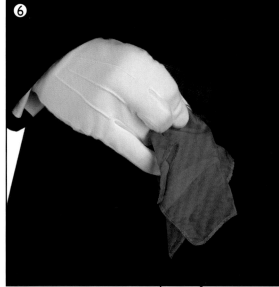
⑥

7. Wave a magic wand over the ring, then ask one of your volunteers to remove the ring from the string. They will be amazed when the ring comes off!

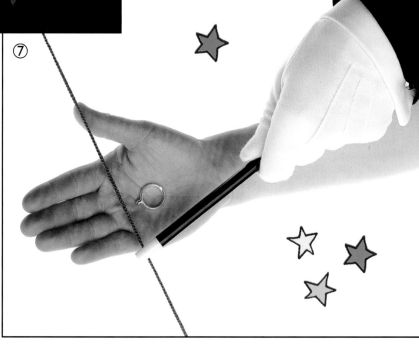
⑦

Coloured Thoughts

Trick a volunteer into tying three different coloured ropes in the same order as you.

Preparation

Before your show, tie one set of ropes together in a special knot. Take the first piece of rope and fold one end into a loop. Tie the loop to one end of the second piece of rope using a simple knot, as shown below. Fold the other end of the second piece of rope in a loop and tie it to one end of the third piece; repeat the knot to tie the remaining loose ends together.

Props box

- Three pairs of different coloured ropes
- A plastic bag

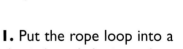

1

1. Put the rope loop into a plastic bag, shake it so the colours are all mixed, and the trick is ready to perform. Show the bag with the three coloured ropes in to your audience and ask for a volunteer. Ask them to tie the second set of ropes together in any order, then to hold them up by one end.

14

2. Look at your volunteer's ropes to see which are the top and bottom colours. Put both hands into the bag and secretly undo the special knot between those two colours – with practice, you should be able to do this very quickly using just one hand.

② ②

3. Take the end of the rope which matches the top rope being held by your volunteer and slowly pull all three ropes out of the bag.

③

4. Your ropes are in exactly the same order as your volunteer's!

Magic Facts

The world-famous Magic Circle is based in London, UK and has a special section, The Young Magician's Club, for people under 18 years old.

Going By Tube

Even an empty card box can be used for a trick!

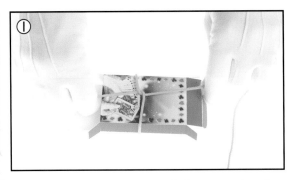

I. Loop the string around the outside of the box or tube. Tie a simple overhand knot.

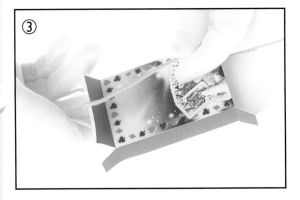

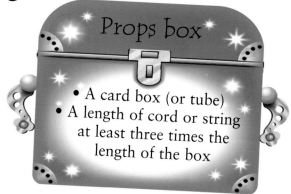

Props box

- A card box (or tube)
- A length of cord or string at least three times the length of the box

2. Push one end of the string into the box and pull it through to the other side.

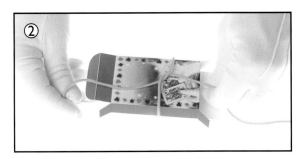

3. As you do this, slide the knot off the box at the same end and push it into the open end. Keep hold of the unthreaded string.

4. As you pull the string through the box, the knot vanishes!

Ribbon Riddle

Use your magic powers to produce a ribbon from nowhere ...

1. Show both hands to your audience, palms forwards. Both are empty ...

Props box

• A ribbon

2. Close your hands inwards and then open them out again – the ribbon appears as you move your hands apart!

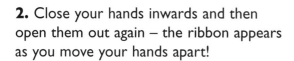

But How?

Secretly wrap the ribbon (use a short length until you have really got the hang of the trick) around your left thumb. Tuck in the end so it doesn't unwind. Keep your hand out of sight until you're ready to perform, and use your right hand to cover your left thumb when you show your hands to the audience. As you close up your hands, keep your left thumb tucked behind your palm. Pull the ribbon undone with your right hand, as you move your hands apart to show the ribbon appearing – as if by magic!

Not a Knot

Your magic wand really is magic, if this trick is to be believed!

1. Tie the two strings around the wand and ask for a volunteer to hold the bottom of the wand. Thread a ring onto the strings at one side, and do the same at the other side.

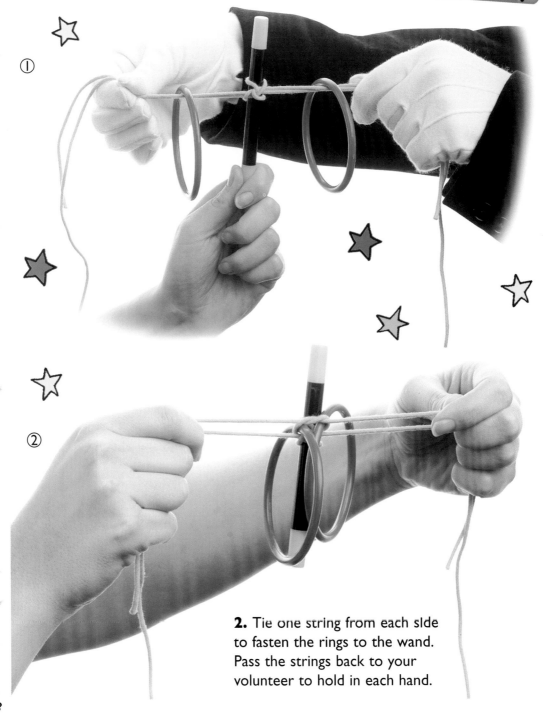

①

②

2. Tie one string from each side to fasten the rings to the wand. Pass the strings back to your volunteer to hold in each hand.

18

3. Now explain that you will remove the wand, and if your volunteer concentrates properly on pulling the strings away from the rings, they will fly loose.

④

4. Say the magic words, 'Jiggery pokery, riddle me ree, think really hard and the rings will be free!' and pull the wand down and out of the strings. The rings come loose!

Trickery Tip

Make your volunteer feel important and encourage them to be part of your performance. The more they smile at the audience, the less they will concentrate on the trick they are holding on to.

But How?

As long as you tie your first knot properly, this trick should be foolproof. Lie your wand across the two strings, then double them over (1). Take one set of strings in each hand and tie them together with one knot (2). Separate them again to pass to your volunteer, making sure that you keep both ends of one string in one hand, and both ends of the second string in the other.

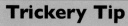

1

2

Impossible Knot

You challenge a member of your audience to tie a knot in a piece of rope without letting go of the ends – when they give up, you show them how it's done!

Props box

• A piece of rope about 1 m long

①

1. Show the rope to your audience, and challenge someone to tie a knot in it without letting go of the ends.

2. When they give up, lay the rope on a table and fold your arms. Pick up one end of the rope with one hand and keeping your arms folded, pick up the other end with the other hand.

②

3. When you unfold your arms a knot magically appears in the centre of the rope!

Swapping Loops

Two different coloured loops of rope change places in a flash!

Props box

• Two coloured pieces of rope

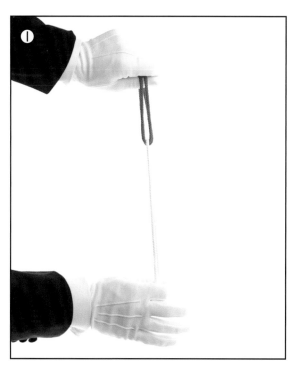

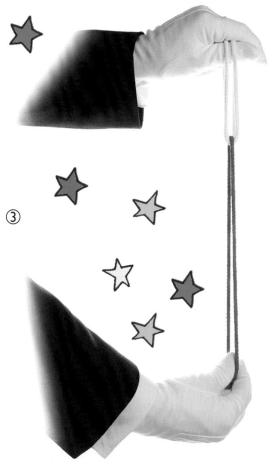

1. Take each piece of rope and tie it in a loop. Fold one loop in half, then thread it through the other loop. Put your left thumb through the two loops formed by the folded rope.

2. With your right hand, take hold of one of the upper loops and quickly pull it downwards.

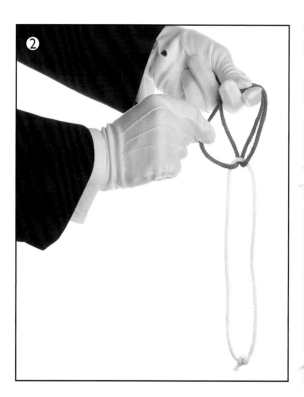

3. Your audience will be amazed to see that the two loops have changed places!

Into the Void

You push a knot into a magic tube and mysteriously it disappears ...

Props box

• A piece of card
  20 cm x 15 cm
• A piece of string
• Glue

1. Make a tube from the card by rolling it up and glue the end down to keep it in shape. When the glue is dry, tie the string loosely around the tube with a simple knot.

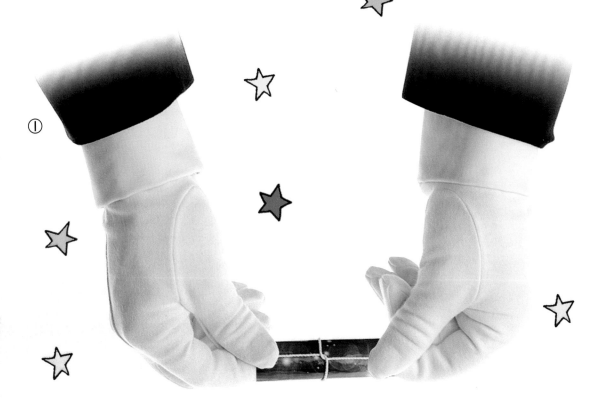

①

Magic Facts

Levitation is a form of magic, in which the magician makes an object float in the air or uses an object to make something else float. Famous acts include – an assistant floating in mid-air, a ball floating around a cloth or a magician hovering a few inches off the floor.

②

2. Take one end of the string and thread it into the tube. Now slide the knot to the end, then carefully slip the knot off and push it into the tube.

③

TA-DAH!!

3. Wave your hand over the tube, say some magic words, then slowly pull the string out from the other end. Amazingly, the knot has disappeared!

23

Solid Through Solid

You make a solid bead pass through a solid sheet of card – impossible? No, just magic!

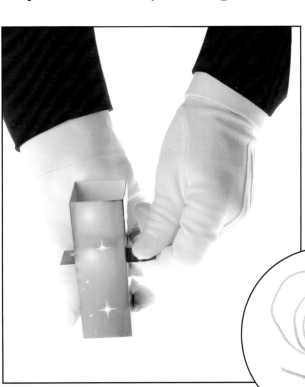

Props box

- A piece of card 12.5 cm x 8 cm
- Scissors • Tape
- Bead and string

Preparation

Copy the template on page 27 onto your piece of card. Push the slide (the saved rectangle) through the tube, then thread the bead onto the string and tie a knot to keep it in place.

1. When you are ready to perform, hold the tube in one hand and the end of the string in the other. Make sure that you hold the tube with the hole towards you, and that you cover the hole with the palm of your hand so that your audience can't see it.

24

2. Lower the bead into the tube until it hits the slide. Move it up and down so that everyone can hear it hitting the slide – they will also be able to see the slide move.

②

③

3. Tell your audience that you are going to make the bead pass through the slide; while you are doing this, tip the top of the tube towards you a little. This will allow the bead to slip out of the hole at the back.

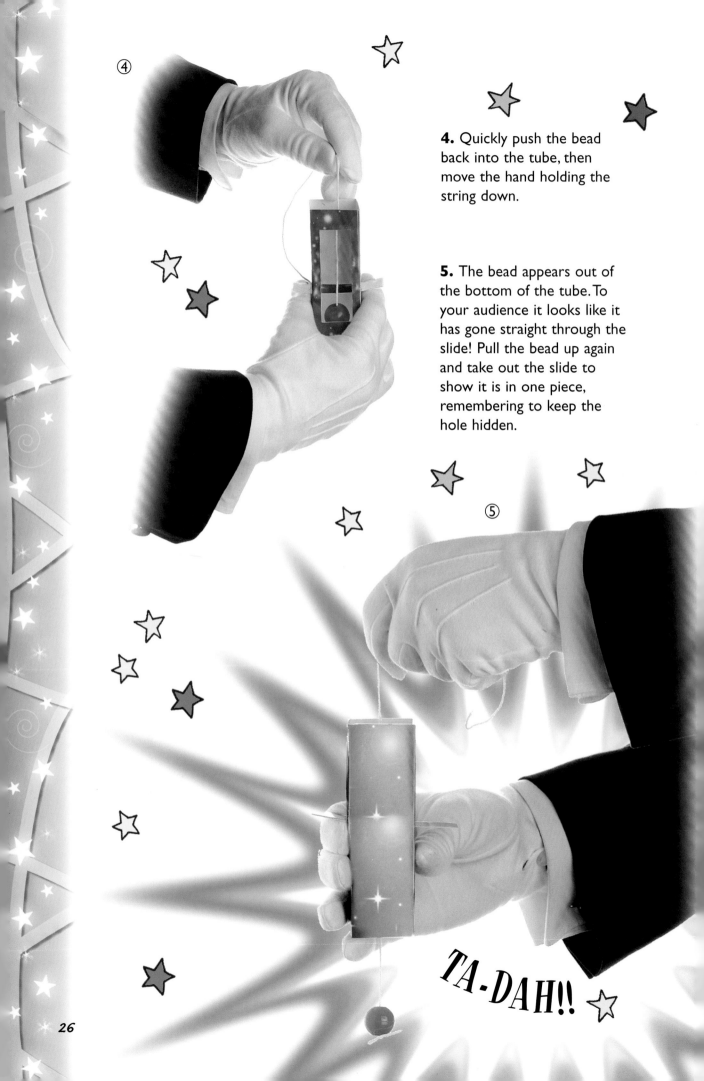

④

4. Quickly push the bead back into the tube, then move the hand holding the string down.

5. The bead appears out of the bottom of the tube. To your audience it looks like it has gone straight through the slide! Pull the bead up again and take out the slide to show it is in one piece, remembering to keep the hole hidden.

⑤

TA-DAH!!

Card Template

Once you have copied the card template onto your piece of card, cut out the marked solid lines, (keeping the large rectangle from the middle). Then fold the tube along the dotted lines marked and glue together.

Magic Facts

The oldest magic organisation is the Society of American Magicians. Houdini, the famous escapologist, was a member and also the president for many years. The Magic Circle, with its specially built headquarters, in London, UK, holds the largest magic library in Europe.

Knots From Nowhere

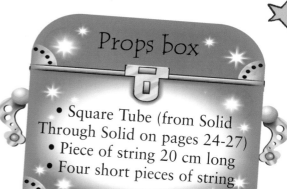

Amaze your audience by producing knots from nowhere with the aid of your incredible magic tube.

Props box

- Square Tube (from Solid Through Solid on pages 24-27)
- Piece of string 20 cm long
- Four short pieces of string

Preparation

Take the tube made for Solid Through Solid (pages 24-27) and remove the slide. Prepare by tying the four short pieces of string onto the long piece. Trim the knots so that the ends are as short as possible, then slide them along the long piece of string until they are about one quarter of the way from one end.

1. Start your performance by holding the string with the knots hidden in your hand.

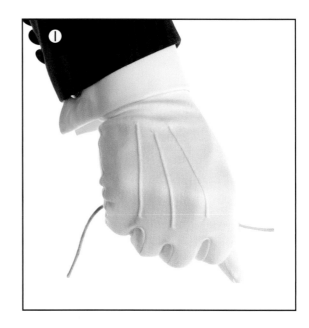

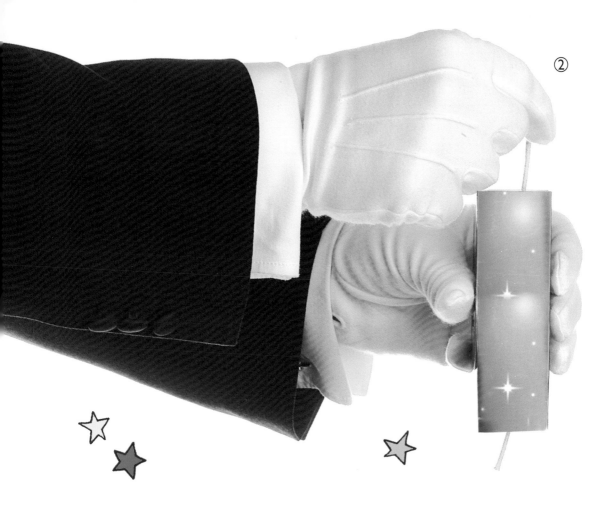

②

2. Holding the tube in your left hand with the hole towards you, push the knotted end of the string into the tube until it appears at the bottom – be careful not to let it go too far, or the audience will see the knots.

3. Turn the tube onto its side, with the hole still facing you. Put your thumb inside the hole so that it touches the knots.

③

29

4. As your right hand pulls the string out of the tube, your left thumb releases one knot at a time so they appear at regular intervals along the string.

④

5. When you finally pull out the string, your audience will see that four knots have now magically appeared!

⑤

TA·DAH!!

The Invincible Rope

You cut an ordinary piece of rope in two – but it must be invincible, because when you open up your hand, it is magically restored to one piece!

Props box

- Scissors
- Piece of rope 10 cm long
- Piece of rope the same type and colour about 1 m long

Preparation
Before your show, fold the short piece of rope in half. Put the rope and the scissors where they cannot be seen by the audience.

1. To perform the trick, show the audience the long piece of rope. Fold it in half and hold it near the top of the loop in your right hand.

①

②

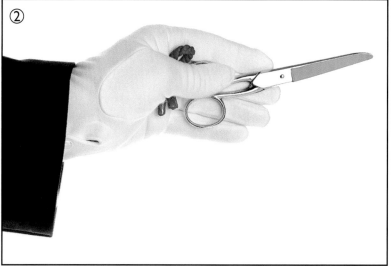

2. Pick up the scissors with your left hand, and at the same time secretly pick up the short piece of rope. Keep this hidden in your left hand.

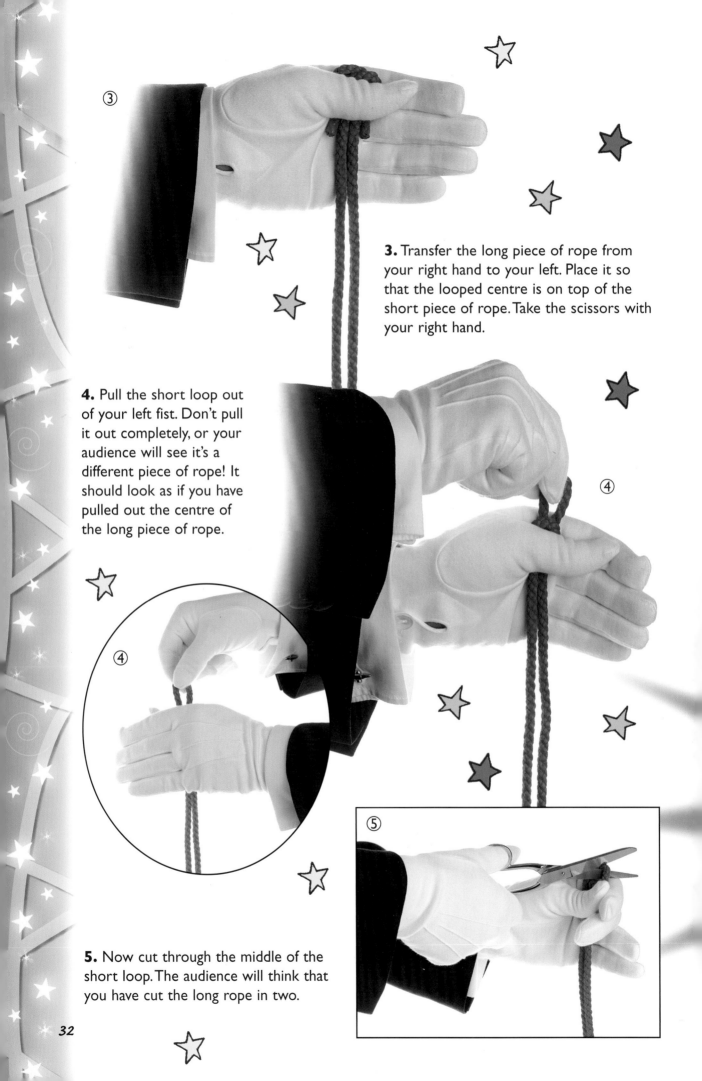

③

3. Transfer the long piece of rope from your right hand to your left. Place it so that the looped centre is on top of the short piece of rope. Take the scissors with your right hand.

4. Pull the short loop out of your left fist. Don't pull it out completely, or your audience will see it's a different piece of rope! It should look as if you have pulled out the centre of the long piece of rope.

④

④

5. Now cut through the middle of the short loop. The audience will think that you have cut the long rope in two.

⑤

6. Cut off the ends of the small loop and throw them away, telling your audience that you are just trimming off the ends of the rope. In reality, this will help you to get rid of the rope at the end of the trick.

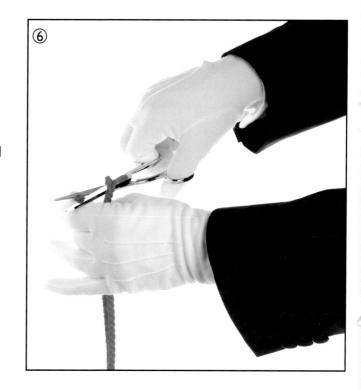

7. Wave the scissors over your left hand, then take the long rope and throw it in the air. Secretly put the remaining ends of the short piece into your pocket.

Incredibly, the long rope has been restored to one piece!

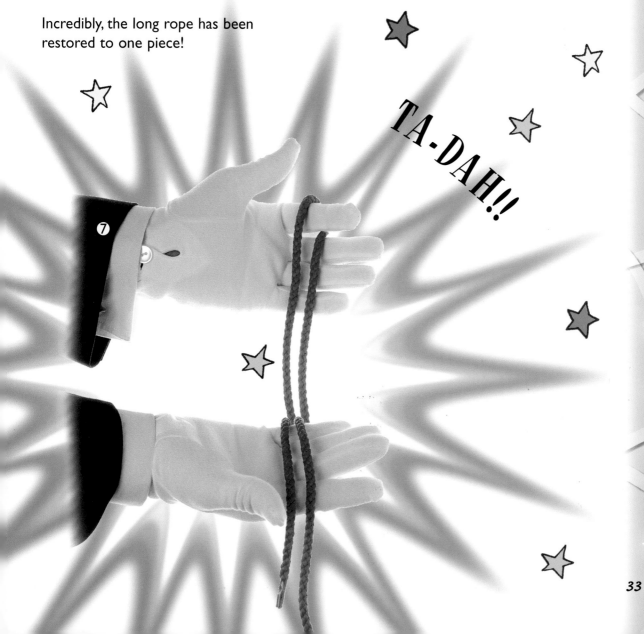

TA-DAH!!

Knotty Business

Practice makes perfect! This trick requires skill but looks really impressive!

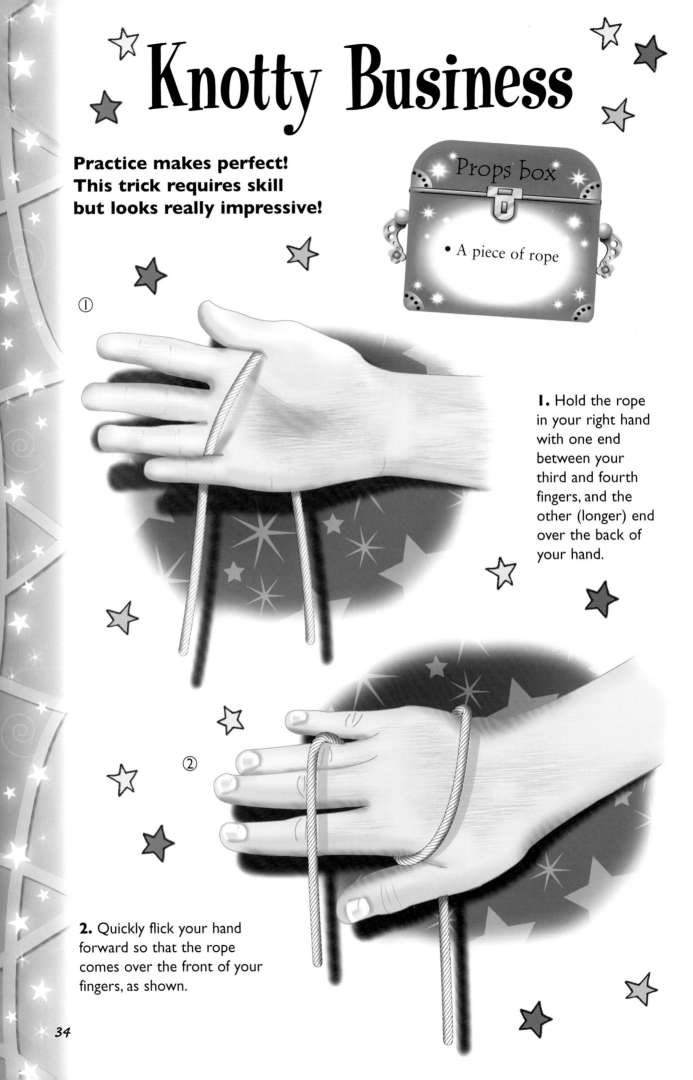

Props box

• A piece of rope

①

1. Hold the rope in your right hand with one end between your third and fourth fingers, and the other (longer) end over the back of your hand.

②

2. Quickly flick your hand forward so that the rope comes over the front of your fingers, as shown.

③

3. Grip the rope with your first and second fingers as you let the rest of the rope fall from your hand. As this happens, a knot is formed.

④

Trickery Tip

Practise with the other hand as well. It looks really impressive if you can hold two pieces of rope and make knots appear in each at the same time!

4. Catch the rope before the knot falls out! This takes a bit of practice, and you may miss the rope completely at first, but you will soon get faster and faster until the knot appears in the rope instantly.

Appearing Knot

If you can't get the hang of 'Knotty Business', cheat with this trick!

Preparation

Before you start, secretly tie a knot in one end of the rope. Put the rope into your left pocket until you are ready to perform.

1. Take the rope out from your pocket, but keep the knot hidden in your left hand. Pass the rope through to your right hand, making sure no one sees the knot.

①

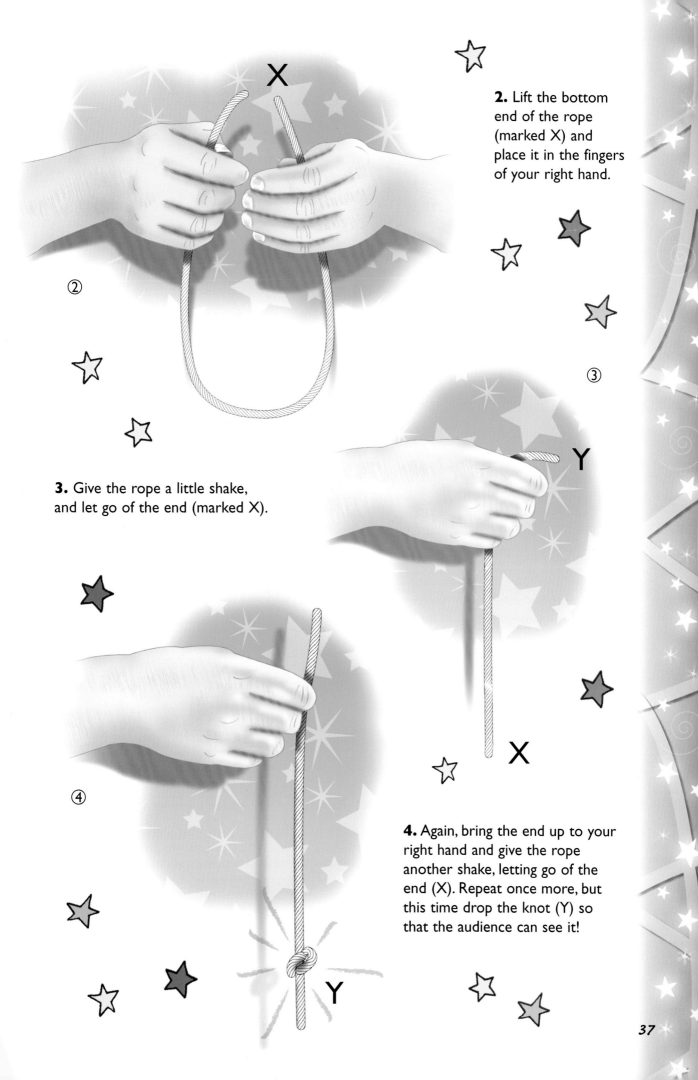

X

2. Lift the bottom end of the rope (marked X) and place it in the fingers of your right hand.

②

③

Y

3. Give the rope a little shake, and let go of the end (marked X).

X

④

4. Again, bring the end up to your right hand and give the rope another shake, letting go of the end (X). Repeat once more, but this time drop the knot (Y) so that the audience can see it!

Y

37

Bead and Rope

Make solid matter pass through solid matter by passing a piece of string through a cardboard loop.

Props box

- A piece of rope 50 cm long
- Two beads, each with a hole in the middle
- A cardboard loop

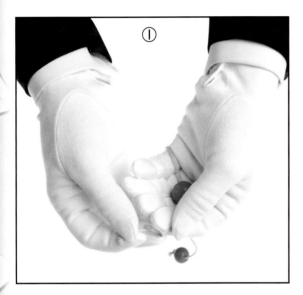

1. Before your show, thread both beads onto the string and tie a knot at each end so that the beads will not come off. Arrange the beads so there is one at each end of the string.

2. To perform the trick, place your loop on the table and show your prepared string to the audience, making sure that you keep one bead hidden in each hand.

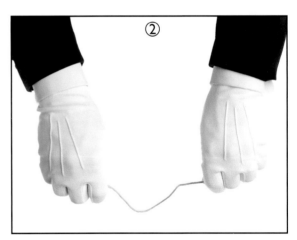

3. As you are preparing to pass the string through the loop, take both beads into your right hand and hold the knot on the loose end of the string with the thumb and first finger of your left hand.

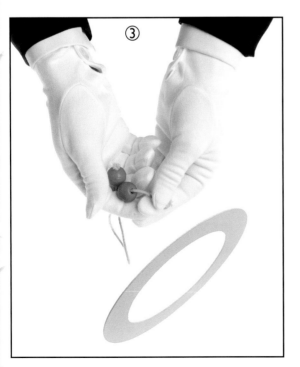

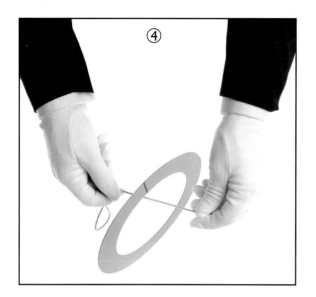

④

4. Now grip the string with the thumb and first finger of your right hand, pass it through the loop and hold the knot with the thumb and first finger of your left hand.

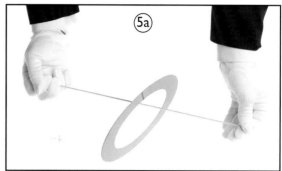

5a

5b

5. Still holding the beads in your right hand, stretch the string through the loop.

Tell your audience that you will now prepare to pass the string through the loop. You do this by bringing the ends of the string together and then stretching it out again. Repeat this a few times.

⑥

6. Bring your hands together one last time and with your left hand grasp the top bead on the string in your right hand. Quickly pull your hands apart.

TA-DAH!!

Although the string has actually passed around the loop, to your audience it will look as if the string has passed through a solid object!

The Incredible Floating Note

Your audience will be amazed as you crumple up a bank note and make it float in mid-air!

Props box
- A piece of very fine cotton
- Sticky tape
- Bank note

1. The secret of this trick is to practise, practise and practise some more before you perform it in front of an audience. To prepare the trick, cut off just over a metre (about 4 feet) of very fine cotton. Tease out a single fibre at one end, and gently pull it away from the other threads. When you have your single thread, don't lose it!

②

①

2. Tape the end of the thread in your performing area, about as high as your shoulder. Then fold a tiny piece of tape over the other end – this will go in your mouth to make the thread taut. The thread is invisible, especially against patterned backgrounds, but try not to work in a brightly lit room. Leave the loose end dangling for later.

3 Now for your performance. Show the bank note to your audience, so they can see that it has no wires attached, and no special tricks hidden within!

4. Take back the bank note, and at the same time pick up the end of your thread and pop it in your mouth. Disguise your action by scratching your face, or pretending to cough and covering your mouth. Tuck the tape between your cheek and gum (as if you're trying to hide chewing gum!).

5. Keep the thread taut as you lift the note to the thread, and slowly fold it in half around it, then crumple it up to keep it in place. Hold the note with your left fingers and rest it on your right palm, then let go completely to leave it floating. Make sure it doesn't bounce on the thread!

6. When the gasps have died down, move your hands around the note to 'prove' that there is nothing holding it up. With practice, you can even learn to make the note move realistically, as if you are floating it from one hand to the other. To finish, unroll the note and pass it around for inspection again – secretly removing the thread from your mouth when no one is looking.

Going Up

This clever elevator appears to move up on two strings all by itself.

Preparation

Make a tube with the card by rolling it up, then slide a paper clip onto the join at one end. Fold both pieces of string in half. Thread the ends of the first piece of string through the loop of the second. Now thread the loop of the first piece of string onto the remaining paper clip.

Props box

• A piece of card 20 cm x 15 cm
• Two paper clips
• Two strings

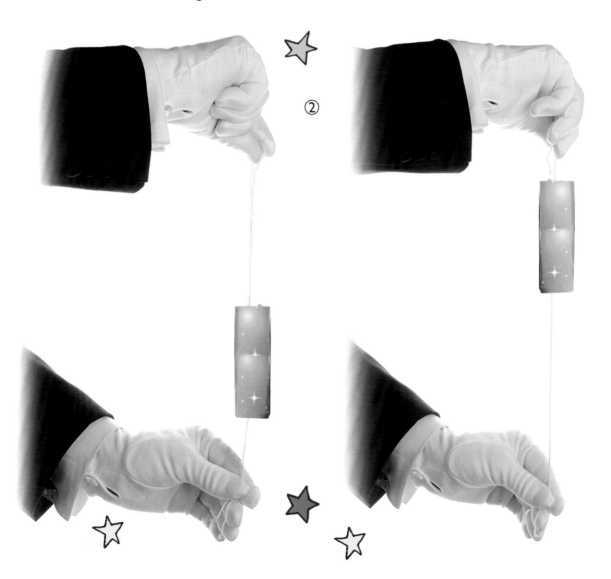

1. Feed the ends of the second string through the tube. Slide the paper clip attached to the first string onto the bottom of the tube, making sure that the loop is hidden inside. You will now have a tube with two sets of strings at either end.

2. Secretly pull on the top and bottom strings and the tube will move upwards all by itself. To reset the enigmatic elevator, simply pull the tube downwards while you hold onto the top strings.

Grandmother's Necklace

You release three beads which you have tied onto a piece of string – but you don't let go of the ends. Amaze your audience with this impressive-looking trick.

Props box

- Two small round beads
- One long bead
- Two pieces of string
- Handkerchief

Preparation

The key to this trick is in the preparation, as the beads are threaded onto the string in a special way. Before your show, fold one string in half and thread the folded end first through one of the small beads, and then through the long bead.

①

1. Now fold the second string in half. Take the folded end and thread it through the loop in the bottom of the first string.

②

2. Fold the loop on the second string over and hold it with your left hand. With your right hand, slide the beads over the two folds to hide them.

45

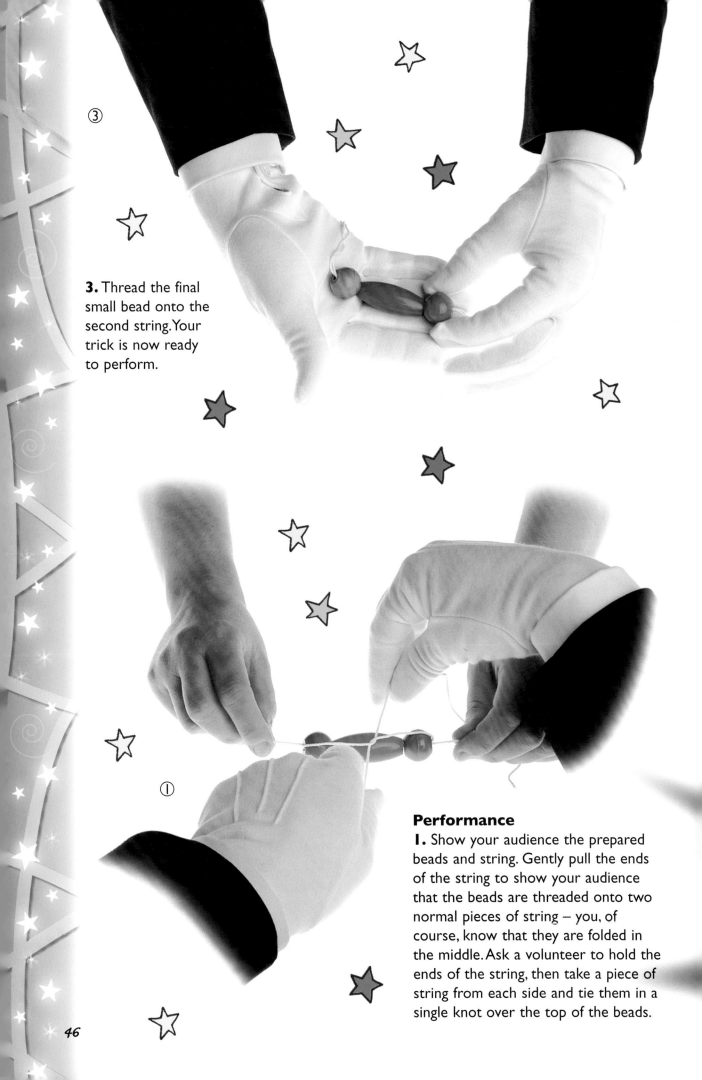

③

3. Thread the final small bead onto the second string. Your trick is now ready to perform.

①

Performance

1. Show your audience the prepared beads and string. Gently pull the ends of the string to show your audience that the beads are threaded onto two normal pieces of string – you, of course, know that they are folded in the middle. Ask a volunteer to hold the ends of the string, then take a piece of string from each side and tie them in a single knot over the top of the beads.

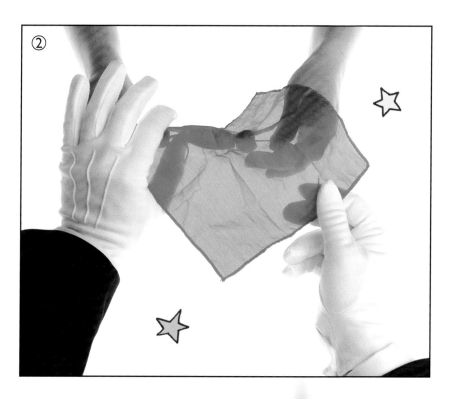

2. Cover the beads with a handkerchief. While you are doing this, secretly slide the middle bead to the right with your left thumb. Ask your volunteer to pull on the ends of the string.

3. Listen for the applause from your audience as the beads release themselves from the string while the ends are still being held by your volunteer!

TA-DAH!!

47

Rope Roller

Make a table tennis ball balance on a single piece of rope.

Props box

• Table tennis ball
• Piece of rope 50 cm long
• Loop of cotton the same length and colour as the rope

1. Before your show, lay the rope and the cotton loop on your table and place the ball on the centre of the cotton loop.

①

2. To perform the trick, take the rope at each end. At the same time, put your thumbs through the cotton loop and stretch it as tightly as you can.

3. Pick up the rope and cotton together. From the audience, it will look as if the ball is balancing on the rope! When you are used to doing the trick, try moving your hands up and down, rolling the ball along the 'rope'.

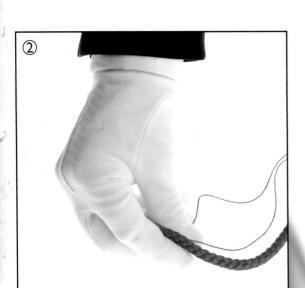

②

TA-DAH!!

③

Tricks

& Illusions

WANDERING
WATER

Tricks
and Illusions

Licensed exclusively to Top That Publishing Ltd
Tide Mill Way, Woodbridge, Suffolk, IP12 1AP, UK
www.topthatpublishing.com
Copyright © 2014 Tide Mill Media
All rights reserved
0 2 4 6 8 9 7 5 3 1
Printed and bound in China

The Rattler

No matter how well your audience follows your movements, no one will be able to keep up with this trick!

1. Place three small boxes on the table and say that one of them contains cocktail sticks. Prove it by shaking them – only one rattles.

Props box

• Elastic band
• Four small boxes, one of which contains cocktail sticks

2. Swap the boxes around really quickly and ask a member of your audience to pick up the one they think contains cocktail sticks.

Magic Facts

For thousands of years, people believed that magicians and sorcerers could control natural forces, such as the weather and diseases.

②

3. Even if your volunteer has followed the boxes intently, the box they choose won't contain any sticks.

③

4. Shake another box to show which one DOES contain cocktail sticks, and then swap them around again. Challenge someone else to pick the correct box. They still won't be able to find one with sticks.

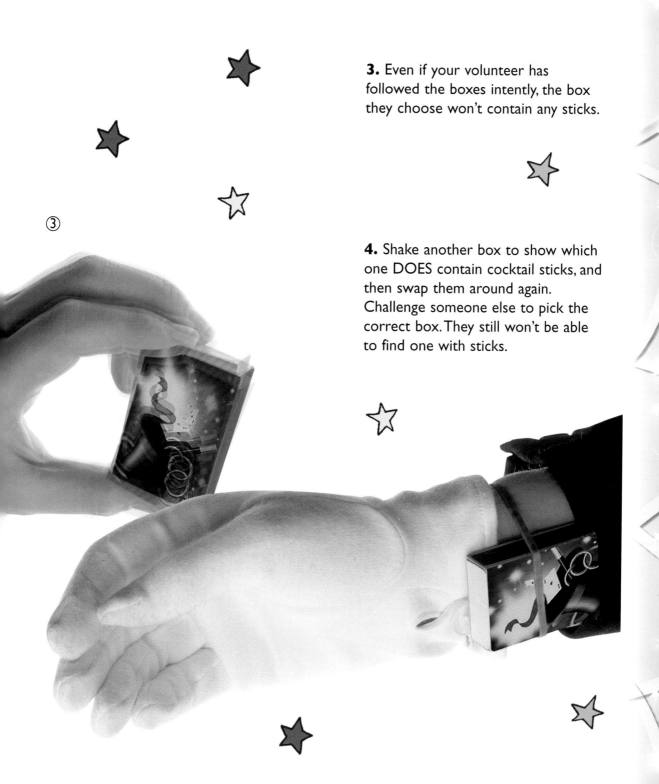

But How?

The secret is that the three boxes are actually empty. In your right sleeve you have an extra box with a few cocktail sticks in it. This is held on your arm with an elastic band or a piece of bandage. When you want to prove a box is empty, shake it with your left hand and there will be no noise. To make a box sound full, shake it with your right hand and the hidden box will make the noise you need.

Wandering Water

Using two plastic cups and two paper bags, make water disappear and reappear!

Preparation

Before your show, carefully cut the bottom from a plastic cup and put this cup inside another one so it looks like a single cup. Practise handling the bottomless cup on its own so it looks as if it is full of water.

1. To do the trick, show the two empty paper bags to your audience. Now pour some water into the paper cup.

2. Place the cup in the first paper bag. Pretend to change your mind, and move the cup into the other bag instead. What you really do is take out only the inner (bottomless) cup and put that in the second bag. Remember, handle it just as if it is full of water.

3. Say some magic words, wave your arms over the bags, and then pounce on the second bag (the one which everyone thinks contains the cup of water), pick it up and crush it between your hands.

4. The cup of water has vanished! Go to the first bag, reach inside and take out the full cup. Pour the water back into a jug to show your audience where the water went!

Linking Clips

You will need paper and paper clips for this simple trick, which will help you get used to talking and performing at the same time.

①

Props box

- Piece of paper
- Two paper clips

1. Fold one-third of the length of paper over to the right. Place a paper clip over this fold to hold it in place.

2. Fold the other end of the paper in the opposite direction, and clip this to the centre piece of paper.

②

3. Quickly pull the two ends of the paper apart.

4. The clips will jump off and magically link themselves together!

③

④

Magic Facts

The word 'magic' comes from a Greek Word 'magika'. Greece had been at war with Persia for centries and Persian priests were known as the 'magosh' in Persian. The term endured in Greek to 'magika', meaning any foreign, unorthodox or illegitimate ritual practice.

Much From Little

Using a pencil and a small box, make a pencil seem longer than it can be!

Props box

- A small box
- Scissors
- A pencil

Preparation

Before you start, carefully cut a small opening in one end of the box. Then, hide a long pencil up your right sleeve.

①

1. When you want to perform the trick, hold the box in your right hand, with one end of the pencil going through the gap in the end of the box.

②

2. With your left hand, open the drawer and reach in to get the pencil.

③

3. Keep pulling and the pencil will appear from inside the box, even though it is obviously too small to contain such a big item.

Magic Facts

In 1584, an English Member of Parliament called Reginald Scot wrote a book called, 'The Discoverie of Witchcraft'. It was written to disprove the idea of witches and show that witchcraft didn't exist. It showed how some magic was done and is thought to be the first textbook on conjuring.

Wonderful Wand

How do you make a wand poke right through the middle of a handkerchief when the handkerchief has no hole in it?

1. This is definitely a trick that needs to be practised in front of a mirror. You need to make sure that everything you do looks convincing to your audience. Hold the end of your magic wand in your right hand, and drape the handkerchief over it.

Props box

- Magic wand
- A handkerchief

①

②

2. Now comes the tricky part. Grasp the material, but make it look as if you are holding the top of the wand through the handkerchief. The picture, right, shows what your audience can see from the front. However, you have some tricky moves to make next, which they can't see ...

③

3. Swivel the wand down towards you and then back up again, so it's behind the handkerchief.

④

⑤

4. Grip the top of the wand with your thumb and wrap the handkerchief around it. Now place your hand under the handkerchief and, with the tip of your forefinger, push the wand upwards.

5. From the front it should look as if the wand is poking right through the middle of the handkerchief! When the wand is all the way through, shake out the handkerchief dramatically to show that there is no hole in it at all!

Just an Illusion

Confuse people into making a seemingly incomplete shape fit together by magic!

Props box

- Tracing paper
- Scissors
- Coloured pencils

Preparation

Carefully trace over and cut out the shape on the next page, following the instructions, and set it out as in the template on page 13.

1. Show it to your friends and tell them to rearrange it so that all the pieces fit together perfectly without a hole. Watch them struggle to achieve this.

①

②

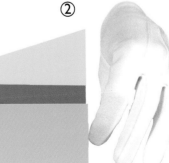

2. Rearrange the shape so that the pieces match the picture at the bottom of page 12. This is the only way to get rid of the hole. Separate the pieces again for your friends to try.

TEMPLATE

Trace over this template, using tracing paper. Colour in the parts in different colours. Then cut out the parts.

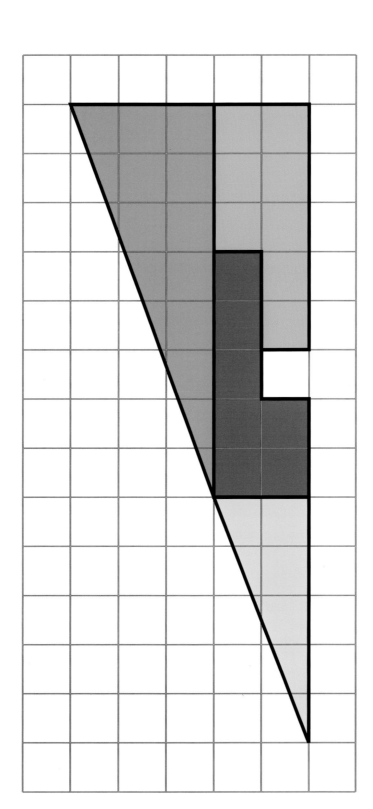

Colour Prediction

Red, green or yellow ... whichever colour is chosen, you can predict it correctly!

Props box

- Three coloured cards
- A pen
- Two envelopes (one large, one small)
- A piece of paper

THIS IS THE COLOUR YOU WILL CHOOSE

YOU WON'T CHOOSE THIS COLOUR

YOU WON'T CHOOSE THIS COLOUR

Preparation

You have to prepare this trick in advance, but once you do it is foolproof. On the red card, write the words THIS IS THE COLOUR YOU WILL CHOOSE on the back. On the green and yellow cards, write YOU WON'T CHOOSE THIS COLOUR on the reverse.

1. You have three cards, each one a different colour. Offer them to your audience for a volunteer to choose one. Let them change their mind as often as they wish, and when they do decide, smile and say, 'I knew you'd choose that one'.

①

2. You also need to prepare two envelopes. Write YOU WILL CHOOSE THE GREEN CARD on a piece of paper and seal it in a small envelope. On the front of the envelope write YOU WILL CHOOSE THE YELLOW CARD. Now seal this inside a larger envelope.

3. Now, no matter which card is chosen, you have an answer prepared. If red is chosen, turn over the cards one at a time to reveal the messages. Keep the red one until last to show that you knew all along it would be chosen.

②

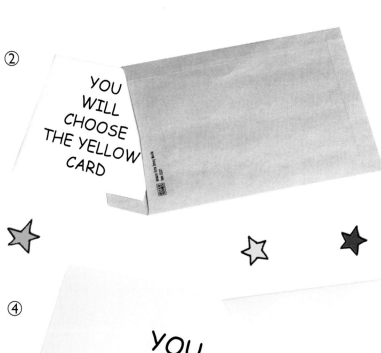

YOU WILL CHOOSE THE YELLOW CARD

④

YOU WILL CHOOSE THE GREEN CARD

4. If yellow is chosen, open the large envelope to show the message on the small envelope inside. If green is chosen, open the large envelope and then open the envelope inside to show the piece of paper.

Trickery Tip

Make sure that your audience cannot see the backs of the cards as they choose their colour to start with. Be careful, too, if you have to open up the small envelope to get the paper, as your audience mustn't see the message written on the back of it.

Mentally Booked

Cover your eyes and still see which side of a book your volunteer is touching.

Props box

- Blindfold or piece of material
- Book

①

1. You need two volunteers to stand in front of your audience, and someone to blindfold you. Ask your first volunteer to open their chosen book at any page.

2. Now they should place their hand on either the left page or the right one, and your second helper can put their hand on the other page.

②

3. Ask the first person to multiply their page number by ten, but not tell you the answer. The second person has to secretly multiply their page number by five. Now ask them to add together their totals and tell you the answer.

Trickery Tip

You can now tell who is touching the righthand page and who is touching the left. If the total number you are given is even, the first person is touching the right-hand page. If the total is odd they are touching the left-hand page.

Ex-Straw-Dinary

Use the power of your mind to make an ordinary drinking straw move ...

1. Place a drinking straw on the table and wiggle your fingers over it. Tell everyone that if you concentrate hard, you can make it move.

①

Props box

• Drinking straw

2. Keep looking at the straw and wiggling your fingers. Suddenly, the straw starts to roll away from you!

②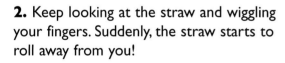

But How?

Perfect your performance and make sure your audience concentrates on the straw and your hands. No one will notice that you are secretly blowing on the straw to make it move!

Spooky Skull

Look at the image of the skull for 60 seconds, without taking your eyes off it and trying not to blink. Then look at the white box to see the skull reappear!

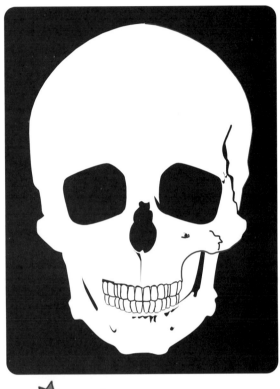

But How?

This is an example of an after-image. These are caused by tired light receptors in our eyes. After being excited by light from the image, they continue to send weak signals to the brain. These weak after-signals are responsible for the faint skull image being visible in the white box.

Magic Facts

Famous magicians of the twentieth century included Dai Vernon, Alexander, Harry Blackstone Senior and Junior, Howard Thurston and Doug Henning. Those in the twentieth and twenty-first centuries include David Blaine, Criss Angel, Penn and Teller and David Copperfield.

Ball of Fire

Look carefully at the Ball of Fire and it will shimmer and move as you watch.

But How?

The shimmer, or flutter, always seems to happen wherever you are not looking. This proves your eye is round and can't focus on the whole picture all at once. Try following the most prominent ring of curves around, and watch it change from a groove to a hump.

Magic Facts

Different categories of magical effects include escape, levitation, vanish, prediction, restoration and production.

Hazy Days

Keep staring at the black dot. After a while, the grey haze around it will appear to shrink.

But How?

Each of our eyes has a region in which there are no receptors (rods or cones), called the 'blind spot'. When you look at the black dot, the grey gradually disappears into your blind spot.

Magic Facts

The vast majority of magicians around the world are micro-magicians (close-up or table magicians). These magicians have to be quick-witted and have excellent sleight-of-hand skills.

Goldfish Bowl

Look at the red eye of the fish on the left for about half a minute. After that, look at the black point in the glass on the right. You should see a fish swimming in greenish water in the glass on the right.

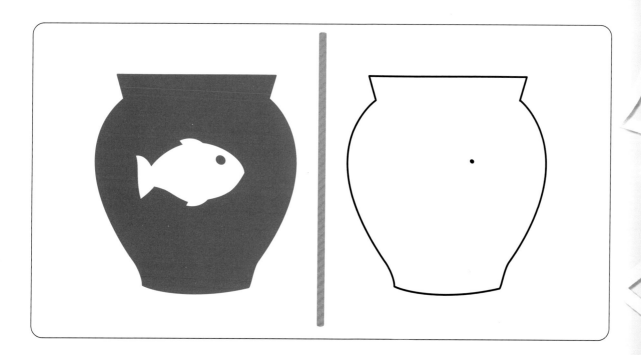

But How?

The explanation for this trick is that the red sensory cells are exhausted because they have been used for a long time. As the colours are mixed, all colours together result in white. However, because red is missing, the result is a mixture of blue and green.

Magic Facts

Some magicians, such as Penn and Teller, include exposing how their tricks are done as part of their performance. A trick is often shown so quickly, that, although the audience knows it is a trick, they cannot follow it and repeat it themselves.

Red, White and Blue

Look at the middle of the upper flag for one minute, without moving your eyes. Then look at the space below it. You will see the red, white and blue flag.

But How?

This is another example of an after-image. After-images always occur in their opposite, or complementary, colour. In this case the opposite of orange is blue, the opposite of green is red, and the opposite of black is white.

Magic Facts

Magicians in the twenty-first century are pushing boundaries and shocking their audiences. In 2003, US illusionist David Blaine spent 44 days in a transparent case in London with only a small amount of water and no food or nutrients.

Vanishing Wand

Make a magic wand disappear in the blink of an eye!

Props box

• Magic wand (or pencil)
• A handkerchief

1. Pass your wand around your audience so they can see it isn't a trick wand.

①

2. Hold it in the air and cover it with your handkerchief. Straighten your forefinger under the handkerchief and let the wand slip down your sleeve and out of sight.

②

3. Now whisk the handkerchief away, remembering to curl your finger back as you remove it. It will look like the wand has disappeared!

③

Trickery Tip

Don't try this trick if you're wearing short sleeves!

Snap

Break a toothpick in two, and then restore it with your magic powers!

Preparation

Before your show, secretly push another toothpick into the hem of the handkerchief. This is the one you must break to make the snapping noise!

Props box

- A handkerchief
- Two toothpicks

①

1. Show the second toothpick to your audience, and place it in the middle of a handkerchief.

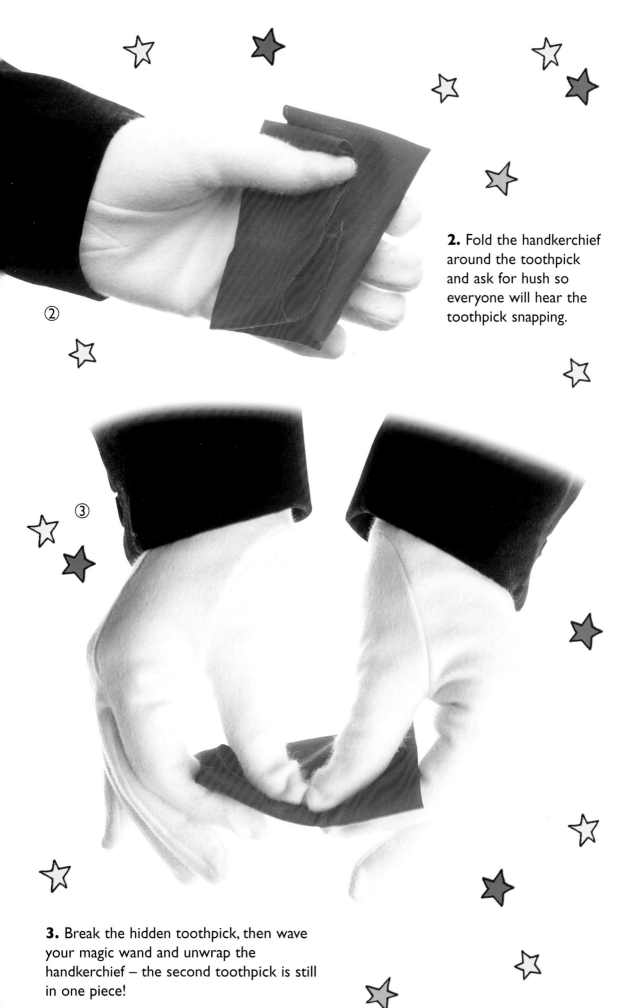

2. Fold the handkerchief around the toothpick and ask for hush so everyone will hear the toothpick snapping.

②

③

3. Break the hidden toothpick, then wave your magic wand and unwrap the handkerchief – the second toothpick is still in one piece!

Dicey Future

Predict the roll of the dice, even when a volunteer shakes them for you!

Props box

- Matchbox
- Glue
- Four identical dice
- Pen and paper
- Envelope

Preparation

Before your show, glue two of the dice into one end of the matchbox drawer. Place the drawer back in the box.

Write down the total of the two numbers that show on the dice and seal the paper in an envelope.

I. Explain that you can make the dice fall as you want them to. Ask someone to place the other two dice into the matchbox. Remember to open the empty end of the box.

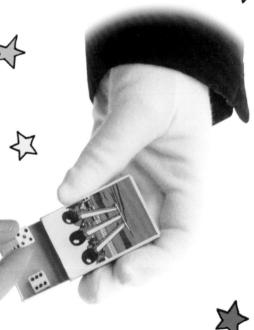

26

2. Ask them to shake the box, and even let them pass it to another member of the audience to be shaken some more.

③

3. Take back the box and open it up to show the glued dice. Ask your audience to add the two numbers on top of the dice.

TA·DAH!!

④

4. Pass the envelope to a member of your audience to open up. Everyone will be amazed at your powers of prediction!

Premonition

 You look into the future and predict the name of a card that will be chosen.

Props box

- Pack of cards
- Pen and paper

1. Ask someone to shuffle the pack.

2. Take the cards back and spread their faces towards you very quickly as you say, 'Yes, they look well-mixed'.

3. What you are really doing is looking for the ninth card from the top of the pack. You must remember this card and you must practise so you can see this card quickly without anyone realising that you are counting up to nine.

4. Put the pack on the table and write down on a piece of paper the card you remembered at the ninth position. Do not let anyone see what you have written, but fold the paper and put it next to the pack of cards.

5. Ask someone to call out any number from ten to 19 and then to deal that number of cards from the top of the pack onto the table.

6. Now, ask for the digits of the chosen number to be added together and that number of cards removed from the cards just dealt. So, if the chosen number was 17, there would be eight cards (1 + 7) removed; if the number was 13, then four cards would be removed.

7. Turn over the next card of the pack and ask someone to read out what you wrote earlier. You will have predicted that very same card.

Mark of the Magician

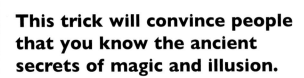

This trick will convince people that you know the ancient secrets of magic and illusion.

Props box

• A lipstick

①

1. Draw a short line of lipstick on the palm of your hand. Make sure it is drawn in the position shown in the picture and crosses the crease at the bottom of your palm.

2. Close your hand tightly. Do not curl your fingers into the fist, but keep them straight, or the trick will not work. When you do this, it will form another mark, which crosses the first line.

②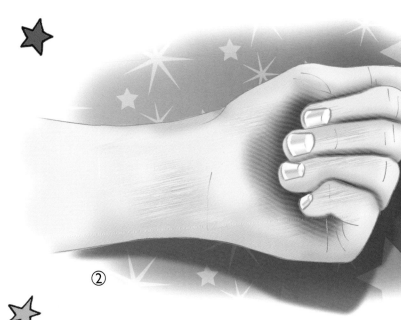

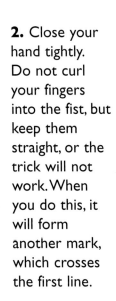

③

3. Draw a short lipstick line on the back of your hand.

4. Now use your fingers to rub out the mark on the back of your hand. Do this quite hard, as if you are trying to rub the mark right through your hand.

④

⑤

5. Open your hand, and show the audience that the mark has 'passed through' your hand to form a cross with the mark you made on your palm. Try to distract the audience with patter or a story during this trick!

Cups and Balls

Amaze your audience with this fast, sleight-of hand illusion, in which three balls mysteriously move between three beakers. Can you see them?

Preparation

Prepare for your trick by stacking the cups together, making sure one ball is trapped in the middle cup and the other three are in the top cup. Show the three balls inside your top cup to your audience.

Props box

- Three coloured cups
- Four identical small balls
- Magic wand (optional)

1. Carefully holding the stack upright, place the three balls in a straight line on the table with your free hand.

①

②

2. Remove the bottom cup from the stack. Place it upside down behind the first ball. Take the second cup (with the hidden ball inside) and quickly turn it upside down behind the second ball, so that nobody can see the ball that is hidden away inside the cup.

③

3. The last cup is placed upside down behind the third ball.

④

4. Pick up the centre ball and place it on top of the middle cup.

5. Drop the left cup on top of it, followed by the right cup. Tap the stack of cups with your magic wand, and lift the stack completely. A ball will remain on the table – this will look as though it has travelled down through the cups on its own.

6. Hold the stack of cups again and repeat the process: one cup behind the first ball, one to cover the second ball and the third behind the last ball. Don't forget to distract the audience with some jokes as you go along.

7. Place the first ball on the bottom of the second cup and drop the other two cups on top, just as you did before in step 5.

⑧

8. Tap twice, and lift the stack ... 'hey presto!' This time there will be two balls left on the table.

9. Once again, put the cups on the table with the centre cup covering the two balls and the third cup behind the remaining ball.

⑨

⑩

10. Place the third ball on the bottom of the centre cup, then drop the other two cups on top, as done previously.

⑪

Trickery Tip

Turn the cups very quickly! This will prevent the hidden ball from falling out. With practice you can do this trick in seconds – the hand really is quicker than the eye.

11. Tap three times, then lift the stack. All three balls now appear to have travelled through the cups!

Colour Match

Let your audience lay out the dominoes however they choose – you will still be able to make correct predictions about them!

Preparation

Take the ten rectangles of card and mark the halfway point. Copy the colour combination from each domino below onto the card rectangles. You'll use these as dominoes for your trick.

Props box

- Card cut into 10 rectangles
- Coloured pencils
- Paper and pen
- Envelope
- Pack of cards

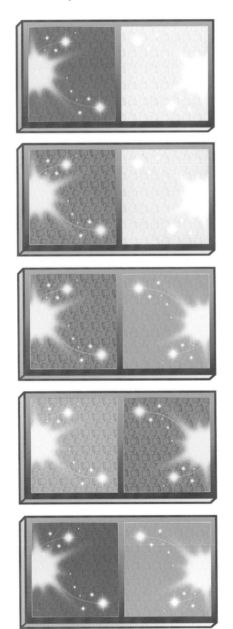

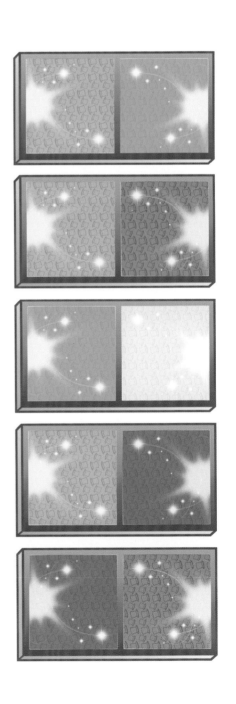

1. Secretly keep one of the dominoes in your pocket. write down its colours and seal the paper in the envelope. Lay the other dominoes in front of your audience.

2. Ask someone to lay out all of the dominoes, colour to colour. Tell them that you have already predicted what colour will be at either end of the line.

3. Pass someone the envelope to open, and they will see that you have written down the correct colours!

ORANGE
BLUE

①

②

③

ORANGE
BLUE

TA·DAH!!

Dead Ringer

Although the string is knotted firmly around the ring, you can break it free!

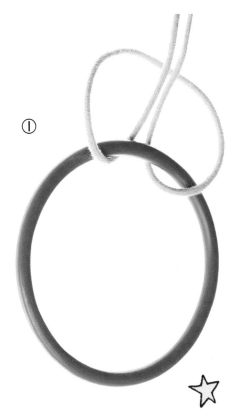

①

1. To perform this trick, you need to prepare for it by tying the knot correctly to start with. Loop the string in half and take the looped end through the ring.

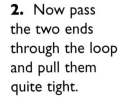

②

2. Now pass the two ends through the loop and pull them quite tight.

3. Dangle the string in front of several members of the audience and ask a volunteer to tug at the ring and prove that it cannot be pulled off the cord.

③

4. To release the ring, use your hands to loosen the knot and slide the loop down and off the ring, as in the picture.

④

5. Ask a volunteer to hold the strings loosely while you cover the ring with your handkerchief. Grasp the ring, say the magic word 'Shalakazar!' and pull the ring completely free, by loosening the knot in the way described in step 4. The audience will be amazed!

⑤

But How?

If you tie the knot correctly to start with, the ring will come loose easily when it is hidden beneath the handkerchief. Loop the string in half and take the looped end through the ring. Now pass the two ends through the loop and pull them quite tight. To release the ring, use your hands to loosen the knot and slide the loop down and off the ring.

Fantastic Folder

This astonishing trick produces more ribbon or even a handkerchief.

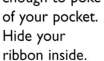

Props box

- Tape
- Two pieces of card
- Paper clip
- Ribbon

Preparation

Take a small piece of card and fold it in half. Tape the sides shut to make a small envelope which will fit into your top pocket, like in the picture below. This needs to have an opened paper clip taped to it, big enough to poke out of your pocket. Hide your ribbon inside.

①

I. Cut another piece of card to about 25 cm x 20 cm (10 in x 8 in). Fold it in half. To show the trick, unfold this card and show both sides to your audience.

②

Trickery Tip

Decorate the folded card with bright patterns to disguise the end of the paperclip so that it won't be seen hanging over the edge.

2. As you show the second side, move the card in front of you and hook the envelope out of your pocket, so that it is secretly hanging behind the folded card.

3. Close the card around the envelope to keep it totally hidden from your audience. Reach into the middle of the folded card, and take hold of the end of the ribbon or handkerchief. Produce it, as if from nowhere, with a flourish and a small bow to your astounded audience.

③

TA·DAH!!

3 In A Row

Magically make all three cups face the same way up, but when your audience tries to do it, it will prove to be impossible!

Props box

• Three small cups

1. The trick is in the preparation. First you need to have all the cups in the same position, as in the picture. The middle cup must be facing up, whilst the other two are facing down, otherwise the trick won't work.

①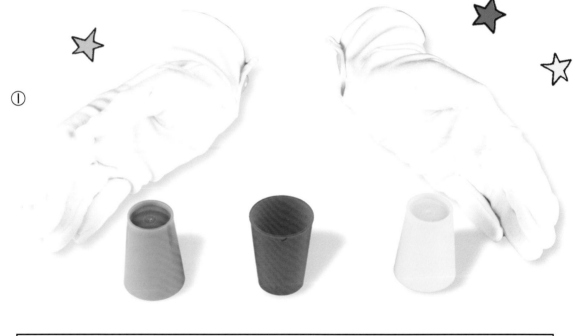

②

2. Once you have set the cups up as in the first picture, you need to show them to your audience and tell them that you are going to turn two consecutive cups over at the same time, but when you've finished, they will all somehow end up facing upwards. Turn the first two cups over, as in the picture above, so that they are facing the opposite way to how they started.

③

3. Now turn the other two over the opposite way so that they, too, are facing the other direction. All of the cups should now be facing upwards. It doesn't really matter in which order you turn the cups over, because they will all end up the same way; facing upwards. Now ask your audience to try it. They won't be able to because of what you do in the next step.

4. When you set the cups up again, make sure the middle cup is facing downwards with the other two facing up, in the opposite way to how you set them up in step 1. Your audience will not be able to turn them over so that they all face upwards. When you show them the trick again, make sure that you set them up as in the first picture, otherwise it won't work. Your audience will be completely baffled when they find they can't do it!

④

Trickery Tip

While you set up the cups, keep up a running patter of jokes to distract the audience from what you are doing. It is important to practise this trick so that you don't forget which cups to turn over during a performance.

A Painless Operation

Ouch! Pick a volunteer and push your wand right into their body!

Preparation

To prepare this trick, make a small tube from coloured paper and glue the edges together. This tube must be just big enough to go over the coloured end of your magic wand.

Props box
• Magic wand
• Coloured paper to match the end of the wand
• Glue

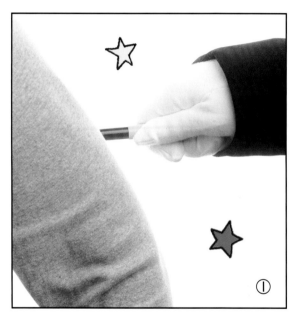

Slide the tube over the end of your wand, so you can't see it.

1. Place the 'uncovered' end of the wand against a friend's body, hiding the coloured part. Your hand must cover the coloured part of the other end, as you move the tube along the wand towards your friend. It looks as if you are pushing the wand into their body. The real wand is hidden by your sleeve.

Trickery Tip

Practise the trick in reverse so you can appear to pull the wand back out without giving the trick away.

Time Flies

Show a wristwatch to your audience, cover it with a handkerchief – and it disappears!

①

Props box

- Handkerchief
- Secret helper

1. Ask to borrow a watch, lie it across your palm, and show it to your audience. Cover the watch with the handkerchief.

2. Now let several people in the room feel beneath the handkerchief to make sure that the watch is still there. Make some mysterious passes over the handkerchief with your hand. Suddenly, whisk away the handkerchief.

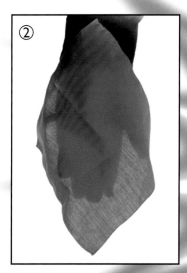

②

③

TA-DAH!!

3. The watch has vanished! What no one else knows is that the last person to feel under the handkerchief is a secret helper, who pretends to feel the watch, but actually takes it away.

Ghost Hunt

Use your magical mental powers to reveal the identity of a spook chosen by a volunteer.

Props box
- Six pieces of card
- Coloured pencils
- A table

Preparation

Before starting this trick, copy the pictures and names of the ghosts on page 48 onto six identical pieces of card.

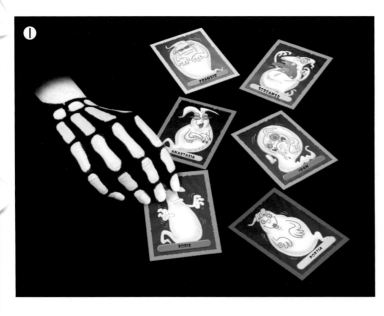

1. Lay the six cards out on the table in any order. Ask a volunteer to choose one of the ghost names and keep it to himself. Explain that you will use your spooky powers to detect the chosen ghost.

2. Ask your volunteer to silently spell out the name of the ghost as you tap the cards one by one. Inform them that they should think of the first letter as you tap the first card. The second letter on the second card and so on. When they reach the last letter of the name, they should shout 'stop!'

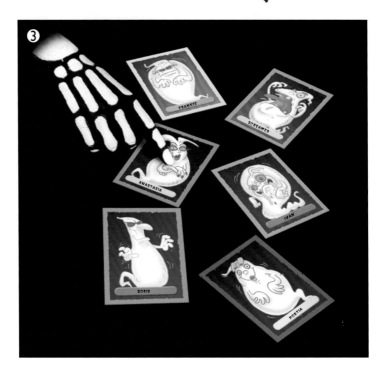

3. Begin to tap the cards with your fingers. Do it very slowly and deliberately, as if concentrating the powers of your mind.

4. The secret of this trick is the order in which you tap the cards, as each ghost has a different number of letters in their name. Your first three taps can be on any card, but your fourth tap MUST be Ivan (there are four letters in his name).

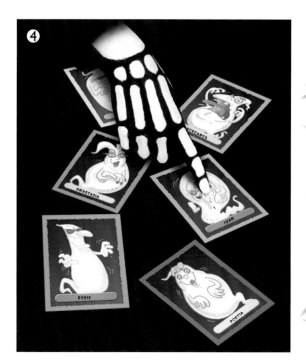

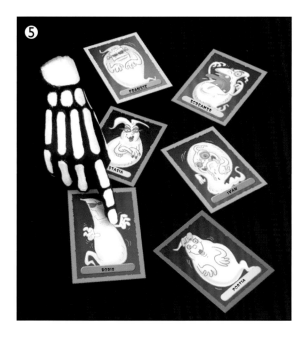

5. After tapping Ivan, you must tap the other cards in the following order: Boris (5 letters), Portia (6 letters), Frankie (7 letters), Screamer (8 letters), Anastasia (9 letters).

6. When your volunteer shouts 'Stop', your finger will be resting on their chosen ghost. Say 'And so the ghost is revealed!' to finish the trick.

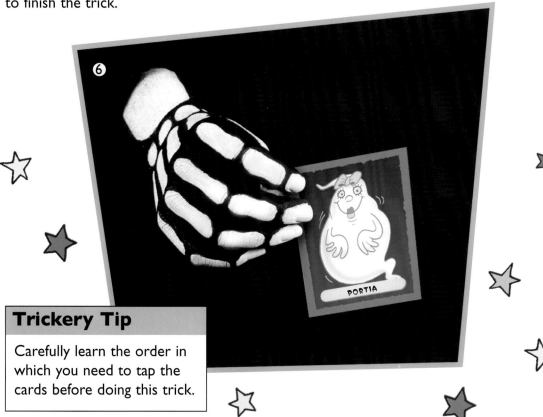

Trickery Tip

Carefully learn the order in which you need to tap the cards before doing this trick.

ANASTASIA

IVAN

BORIS

PORTIA

FRANKIE

SCREAMER

Conjuring Tricks

TRAVELLING
COIN

Conjuring Tricks

TOP
THAT™

Licensed exclusively to Top That Publishing Ltd
Tide Mill Way, Woodbridge, Suffolk, IP12 1AP, UK
www.topthatpublishing.com
Copyright © 2014 Tide Mill Media

Down Under

Cards are mixed up, but they stay in the same order. You will amaze yourself with this trick!

1. Take ten cards, ace to ten, and arrange them in numerical order. Turn the cards face-down and say you are going to deal the cards onto the table. Choose a volunteer.

2. Deal one card at a time, unless the volunteer says 'down under'. When that happens, take the card you are about to deal, place it under the next card, and put both cards down together.

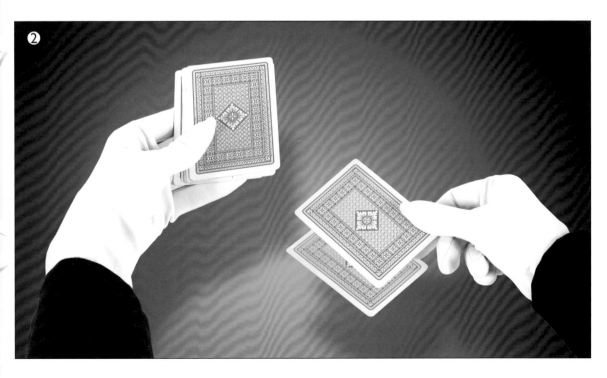

2

3. Continue to deal through the pack like this, dealing one card at a time except when the volunteer calls out 'down under' – which can be at any time.

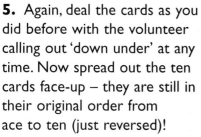

4. When all ten cards are on the table, pick them up and say 'Let's do that again to make sure they are well mixed.'

5. Again, deal the cards as you did before with the volunteer calling out 'down under' at any time. Now spread out the ten cards face-up – they are still in their original order from ace to ten (just reversed)!

Royal Night Out

The four royal families get mixed up dancing at a party, but magically sort themselves out again in time to go home!

Props box

• A pack of cards

1. Take the king, queen, jack and ace of spades and lay them out in a row on the table. Say, 'One day the Spade royal family decided to hold a party.'

①

2. 'They invited the Heart royal family, the king, the queen, the prince and the princess (ace).' Place each of these on top of the cards on the table as you talk.

3. 'And the king, queen, prince and princess of clubs.' Put each of the club cards on top of those on the table.

4. 'They even invited the Royal House of Diamonds to the party.' Put the king, queen, jack and ace of diamonds on top of the others.

④

⑤a

5. Put the four piles together, one on top of the other, and then turn them face-down. 'And they danced the night away.' As you say this, keep cutting the pile of cards to give the impression that they are being well mixed (do not shuffle them).

⑤b

6. Now deal the cards out into four face-down piles as you say, 'At the end of the evening, the carriages arrived and the royal families each went home to their own palace.' Turn each pile over in turn and spread them out on the table to show that each of the four suits have grouped themselves together.

7. 'The Diamond family went home to their palace, the Clubs to theirs, the Hearts to theirs and the Spades went to bed.' Pick up all the cards and put them back into the box.

That's Magic!

Magic words are used to find a card that someone is only thinking of.

Props box

• A pack of cards

1. Deal three piles of seven cards. Turn the cards over and spread out the cards in each pile. Ask a volunteer to think of any card and tell you which pile it is in.

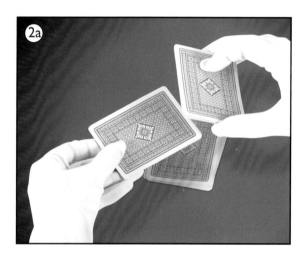

2. Put the three piles together, with the chosen pile between the other two. Deal the cards into three piles once again.

3. Spread the cards out face-up and ask which pile now contains the 'thought-of' card. Put the three piles together, again with the chosen pile going between the others.

4. Deal out the cards again and then repeat step 3.

5. Now deal the cards onto the table, one at a time to spell out the words 'that's magic', one card going down for each letter. Ask the volunteer to name the card being thought of. Turn over the next card – it is the chosen card! Now that's magic!

Round the Clock

A magic clock reveals the identity of a chosen card.

Props box

• A pack of cards

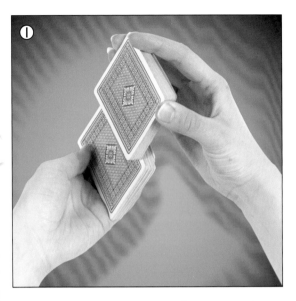

1. Ask a volunteer to shuffle the cards and then hand the pack back to you.

3. Turn away as you say that you want the volunteer to take any number of cards from the small pile and put them in a pocket or sit on them.

4. The rest of the cards are then to be shuffled and one card chosen. This card must be remembered, placed on the bottom of the pile and the pile then put back on top of the pack.

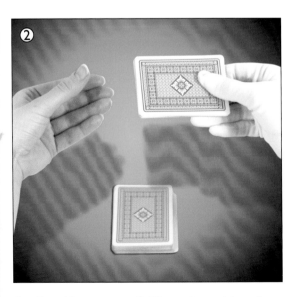

2. Quickly count off 13 cards and hand them to the volunteer. Do not say anything about the number of cards in this pile. Put the rest of the pack on the table.

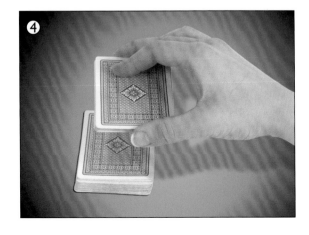

5. You now turn back to face the audience as you say you are going to use the cards to make a clock face. Deal 12 cards into the positions of the numbers on a clock, starting at 12 o'clock and then moving around in an anti-clockwise direction. This means that the second card goes at the 11 o'clock position, the third at 10 o'clock and so on around the clock face.

6. Ask the volunteer to count how many cards were removed from the pack at the start of the trick. You then count to that position on the clock face – so, if 5 cards were taken, you count to five o'clock, if eight cards were taken, you go to 8 o'clock, and so on.

7. Ask for the name of the card that was chosen and turn over the card where you stopped counting in step 6.

8. It is the chosen card!

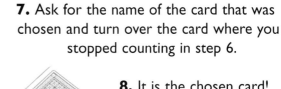

Telephone Telepathy

You read the mind of a friend over the telephone!

1. Before ringing a friend, write the numbers 1 to 26 on a sheet of paper.

2. Ring your chosen friend and ask them to get a pack of playing cards.

3. You now ask your friend to follow your instructions: 'Shuffle the cards and then cut them into two roughly equal piles.'

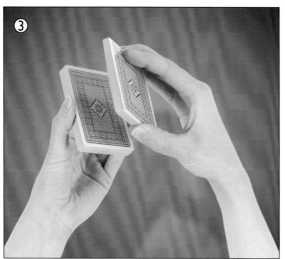

4. 'Pick up one pile and push the other one to one side.'

5. 'Now count the number of cards in your chosen pile, but do it quietly so I can't hear.'

6. 'Have you done that? Good. Now, whatever number you have, add together the two digits of that number. If, for example, you have 21 cards, add the 2 and the 1 to get 3.'

7. 'Take that number of cards from your chosen pile and discard them.'

8. 'Now think of any number between one and ten. Take that number of cards from your pile and put them in your pocket. Again, do it so I cannot hear how many you have taken.'

9. 'Next, I want you to count down the same number of cards in what is left of your pile and memorise the card at that position.'

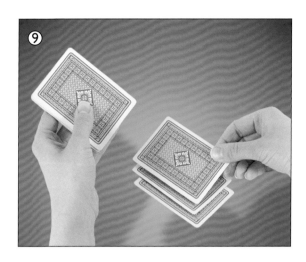

10. 'I think you will agree with me that there is no way I can know how many cards you have in your pocket or what card you are thinking of. So, I want you to do just one more thing.'

11. 'I want you to pick up your chosen pile and deal the remaining cards out one at a time, calling out their names as you do so.'

12. As each card is named, write it down on your numbered list, starting with one and working your way down.

13. When your friend has finished, look at the number against the last card called – that is the number of cards in your friend's pile.

15. Let's say, for example, your list shows that there are 13 cards in your friend's pile. Subtract 13 from 18 and you get 5, so the fifth card's name is the chosen card.

16. You can now tell how many cards are in the pile, how many cards are in your friend's pocket, and, even more amazingly, the card that your friend is thinking of!

14. You now have to do a quick calculation. If the number of cards is less than 9, subtract the number from 9. If the number is between 9 and 17, subtract it from 18. And if there are more than 18, subtract the number from 27. The number you are left with will tell you what number on your list to look at. This will tell you the card your friend has memorised.

Coin Vanisher

Make a coin – or any small object – vanish into thin air before your audience's eyes!

1. Secretly place a small elastic band over the thumb and first two fingers of your left hand.

Props box

- A small elastic band
- A handkerchief
- A coin

①

2. Lay the handkerchief over your hand and open your fingers underneath, stretching the band. Show a coin and push it into the centre of the handkerchief, so you can hold it with the fingers of your left hand. Say some magic words, then grab one corner of the handkerchief and shake it in the air.

TA·DAH!!

③

②

3. It appears that the coin has vanished, but really it is hidden in a secret pocket in the handkerchief made by the elastic band.

Coin Vanish

This illusion is useful to know for other tricks where you have to make a coin or small object disappear.

①

1. Hold a coin by its edge as in the picture. Keep your free fingers out of the way so the coin can be seen clearly.

②

2. Place the coin against the open palm of your left hand, and close your left fingers over it.

③

3. Keep hold of the coin with your right hand, but allow your fingers to relax until they rest on the back of the fingers of your left hand.

④

4. Now move your left hand away with your fingers hiding the coin. Reach into your pocket with your right hand and bring out your magic wand.

Magic Facts

With the lack of books during the Renaissance period, illusionists passed the secrets of their trade from one generation to another.

15

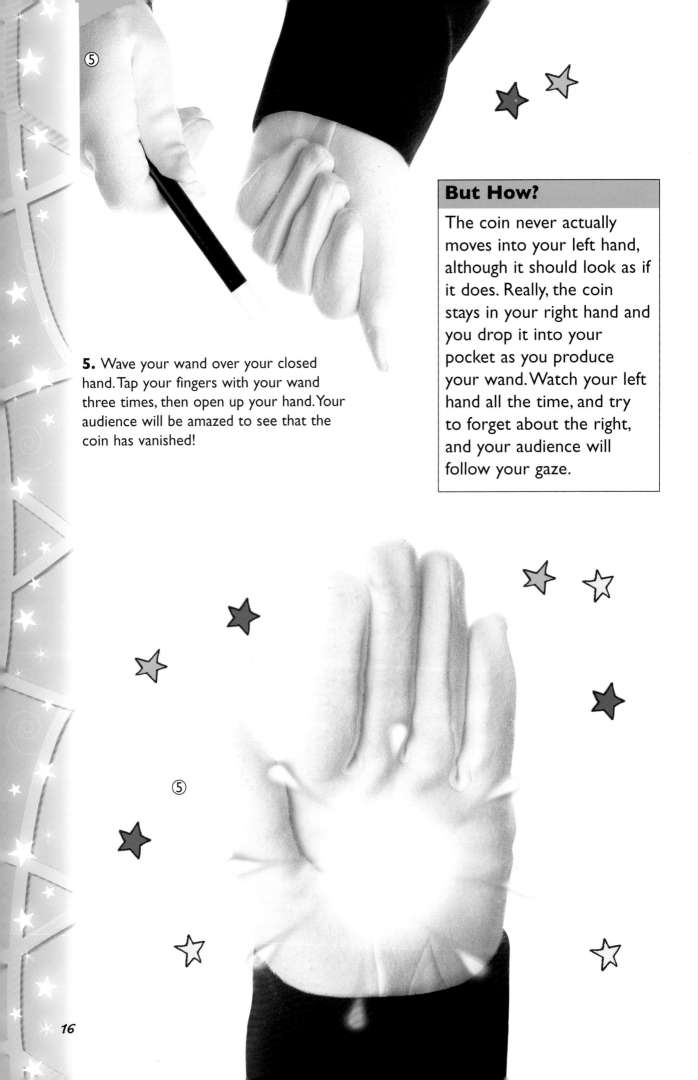

⑤

5. Wave your wand over your closed hand. Tap your fingers with your wand three times, then open up your hand. Your audience will be amazed to see that the coin has vanished!

But How?

The coin never actually moves into your left hand, although it should look as if it does. Really, the coin stays in your right hand and you drop it into your pocket as you produce your wand. Watch your left hand all the time, and try to forget about the right, and your audience will follow your gaze.

⑤

Magic Marker

A marked coin moves from one pocket to another!

1. Ask if anyone is prepared to make a donation to your magic fund by giving you a coin.

①

2. Before you take the coin, pass someone a marker pen and ask them to make a secret mark on the coin.

②

3. Take the coin in your left hand and pretend to put it in your left pocket. Behind your back, swap the coin into your other hand. To distract everyone's attention, make a show of asking for your marker pen back. Now put your right hand into your right pocket and – surprise surprise! Pull out the marked coin from your right pocket!

③

Trickery Tip

The more you joke about getting your pen back, the less people will notice that you are swapping the coin from hand to hand.

Money on the Move

Move a coin from underneath a glass – without touching it! This trick requires slick sleight-of-hand and quick thinking!

Props box

- Two large coins
- Tablecloth • One small coin
- One glass • Handkerchief
- Magic wand

1. Put two large coins on a table (which must have a tablecloth on it), a little way apart. Put a small coin between them and cover it with a glass, so the rim is resting on the two outer coins.

2. Cover the glass with a handkerchief. Explain that you are going to get the coin out from underneath the glass without touching anything. Wave your wand over the glass and concentrate all of your magical powers on the coin.

Magic Facts

Harry Houdini (real name, Ehrich Weiss), was one of the world's most famous escapologist magicians. Born in 1874, Houdini became well known for performing daring stunts and tricks. Some of his most famous acts include escaping from handcuffs and also a straightjacket.

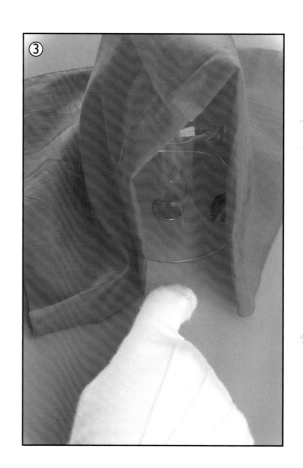

3. What your audience doesn't know is that you are secretly scratching the tablecloth behind the glass with your other hand. Use the first finger of one hand, but distract the audience's attention with your wand-waving and magic words.

4. When you remove the handkerchief, the coin is outside the glass! You will have to practise this beforehand to see how long it takes for the coin to move from underneath the glass as you scratch.

Travelling Coin

Use your magical powers to make a bronze coin and a silver coin magically change place.

Props box

- One silver coin
- Two identical bronze coins
- Two tissues (different colours) • Magic wand

①

1. Prepare for your trick by secretly hiding one of the bronze coins up your sleeve, and putting your wand in your pocket.

②

2. Show the other two coins and the tissues to your volunteers and ask them to inspect them closely. While they are doing this, let the concealed bronze coin slip from your sleeve into your hand.

3. Place a tissue over a silver coin. When hidden, secretly swap it for the bronze coin in your palm. Pick up the bronze coin in the tissue and give it to one of your volunteers to hold. Keep the silver coin hidden in your hand.

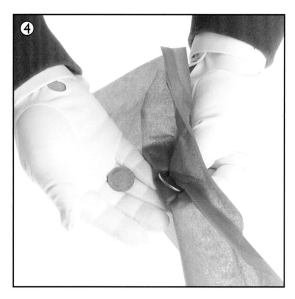

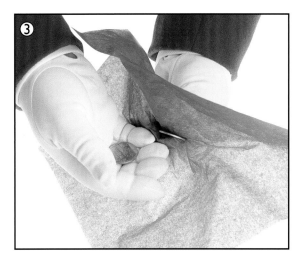

4. Take the other tissue and the second bronze coin. Repeat step 3, switching the bronze coin for the silver one, keeping the bronze coin hidden in your hand.

5. Take your magic wand from your pocket, leaving the bronze coin behind. Announce that you are going to make the coins travel. As each volunteer opens their tissue, they will be amazed to see that the coins have swapped places.

Body Language

It seems like magic, but you need a secret accomplice to make this trick work ...

Props box

- Six coins
- A secret accomplice

1. Turn your back so that someone in your audience can choose one of the six coins on the table. Point out that you can't possibly know which they choose.

①

2. Turn to face the table, sneak a look at your secret helper, and instantly you can point to the chosen coin. Amazing!

②

But How?

Lay the coins on the table as you see in the picture. Think of them as a face, with two eyes, two ears, a nose and a mouth. All your accomplice needs to do is touch the appropriate part of their own face, to let you know which coin was chosen.

★International Magic

Identify the very coin that was chosen while your back was turned ... your audience won't have a clue how you did it!

Props box

- A selection of foreign coins
- A paper bag

1. Put some foreign coins in a paper bag and ask someone in the audience to pick out one coin, without letting you see it.

2. Turn your back and ask them to pass around the coin so that everyone can have a good look. Turn around to let them drop the coin back in the bag.

3. Reach inside the bag and pull out their chosen coin. This should be easy, as it will be warmer than all the others after being handled so much!

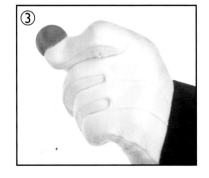

High Glass Act

Matchstick or cocktail stick tricks are great fun to play since they are far more difficult to solve than they look!

①

1. The aim of this trick is to get the coin 'out' of the 'glass' in only two moves. Arrange the matches and coin, as shown.

②

2. Your final move should also ensure that the glass shape is complete again. To start, move the base of the glass to the right.

③

3. Now move the match on the left over to the right and below the base of the glass, as shown in the diagram above.

4. The coin is now out of the glass and the glass has kept its shape (although it is now upside down!). Now challenge your friends to see if they can do it. Once they have given up, run through the sequence of moves with them!

④

TA·DAH!!

Warning!
Ask before you perform this magic trick with matches. Never leave matches near young children. Never use live matches.

Warning!

Ask an adult before you perform this magic trick with matches. Never leave matches near young children. Never use live matches.

Copper Atomizer

Your audience will groan as they think you've lost their money . . . until it reappears!

Props box

• A sheet of paper
• A coin

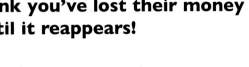

①

1. Fold the piece of paper and place the coin inside the fold. Make sure there is at least 2 cm from the top of the coin to the open end.

②

2. Fold the left edge in over the coin, then repeat with the right edge.

③

3. Turn the paper over and fold down the top edge. It looks as if the coin is securely folded in the paper, but the top edge is actually open!

4. Hold the paper in your right hand with the open edge at the bottom. Release the grip on your fingers, and the coin will secretly slip out of the paper and into your hand.

④

④

⑤

5. Keep the coin hidden in your hand as you tear the paper into pieces. The coin has vanished! Put your right hand in your right pocket to reveal the coin – which has magically reappeared!

Guessing Game

With this amazing trick, you can make three true statements about how many coins a volunteer will pick from a bowl of coins!

Props box

• A bowl filled with coins – the more coins the better

①

1. Ask a member of the audience to take a few coins from the bowl, then you do the same. You must make sure you take a few more than the volunteer.

2. Tell the volunteer not to count their coins yet, but count yours. When you do this, mentally subtract a number under five – this will be the number you use in your second statement – from your total. The number you are left with is the number of coins you will use in your third statement.

②

3. Then make your three statements:

• 'I will have the same number of coins as you in my pile.'

• 'I will have ... (insert number of coins for second statement) more than you.'

• 'I will have enough to make yours ... (insert number of coins for third statement).'

③

④

4. Let them count their coins. Let's say your volunteer had fourteen. You say 'as many as you', and count out fourteen coins. 'And then I said six more.' Count six more coins down. 'And you will end up with fifteen.' Count out your last coin to make the volunteer have fifteen!

Prediction Power

With apparent ease, you will be able to pick the envelope that contains a chosen coin, that matches a previously-written statement!

①

Props box

• Six different coins
• Six identical white envelopes
• A white candle • A pencil
• A piece of paper
• An adult assistant

Preparation

Ask an adult to help you light the white candle and drip a little bit of wax on one of the envelopes.

1. Lay out the six coins. Explain to your audience that when you turn your back, you want them to choose a coin and write its denomination (value) on the piece of paper.

②

2. Without looking, pass the wax-marked envelope to an audience member and ask them to seal the chosen coin inside.

3. Now ask another audience member to place the other coins into the identical envelopes, so there is only one coin in each envelope, and mix up all the envelopes.

4. Bring the envelopes close to your eyes, so that you can see which envelope has the wax mark. Show the audience the six envelopes and tell them which has the chosen coin hidden in.

5. Separate the marked envelope that contains the chosen coin. Pass it to an audience member and ask them to open it. Check the coin against the value written earlier on the piece of paper. Everyone will be in awe to see the value of the coin and the value written on the paper are the same!

⑤

Magic Sums

Double your money with this quick and easy trick!

Preparation

Place three of the coins under the cover of the magazine or book. Put it on the table until you are ready to perform the trick. Place the remaining three coins on the cover of the magazine or book.

Props box

- Six identical coins
- A magazine or book

1. Carefully pick up the magazine or book with one hand, whilst showing your other hand to the audience to prove that it is empty. Tilt the magazine or book so the coins on the cover fall into the hand holding it. The hidden coins under the cover should also discreetly fall into your hand holding the magazine or book.

①

2. Say a few magic words. When you open your hand that was holding the magazine or book, there will be six coins instead of three! Amazing!

②

TA·DAH!!

Counting Coins

This is a great party trick, or one for when you're at school and want to impress your friends! It may seem difficult, but you only need to practise a few times to remember how to work out which is the covered coin. Your friends will be amazed!

Props box

• At least five coins
• A table

1. Drop the coins onto the table and count how many are 'heads' up.

2. Ask a volunteer to turn over five coins without you seeing, saying 'turn' each time they do so. Whenever they say 'turn', add one to the number you counted in step one.

3. Ask the volunteer to slide one coin away and cover it up, again without you seeing.

③

4. This is the tricky part. If the number you are left with is EVEN, count how many coins are left 'heads' up. If this is also an even number, the covered coin will be 'tails' up.

On the other hand, if there is an odd number of 'heads', then the covered coin will be 'heads' up.

If the number you are left with is ODD, count the 'heads' coins again. If there is an odd number of them, the covered coin is 'tails' up.

If there is an even number of 'heads', then the covered coin will be 'heads' up. Easy!

④

Trickery Tip

All you have to do is remember:
Same + Same = Tails
One Even + One Odd = Heads

Cover Up

You will need a friend to help you pull off this vanishing trick!

Props box
- A handkerchief
- Secret accomplice

Preparation

Make sure you have a volunteer to help you perform this trick, and make sure that you position your accomplice to be the last person at your right side.

①

1. Borrow a coin and place it under the handkerchief. Tell your audience that you will now make the coin disappear, but to be sure it's still there, ask a few people to feel it.

2. Holding the coin through the handkerchief, ask a few people, starting at your left, to touch the coin under your handkerchief. The last person to touch the coin should be your chosen accomplice.

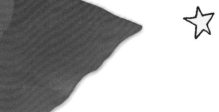

②

3. Instead of inspecting the handkerchief, your accomplice secretly takes the coin away from under it and hides it in their pocket. Then, when you take away the handkerchief you can reveal that the coin has vanished!

Trickery Tip

Make sure that your accomplice looks as surprised as everyone else when you reveal that the coin has vanished. But make sure they don't overdo the surprise and give the game away!

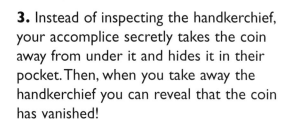

③

37

Changing Coins

Turn a copper coin into a silver one in front of your audience's eyes!

Preparation

Make two copies of this template – this will be the wallet.

Props box

• A copper coin
• A silver coin • Paper
• Scissors • Glue

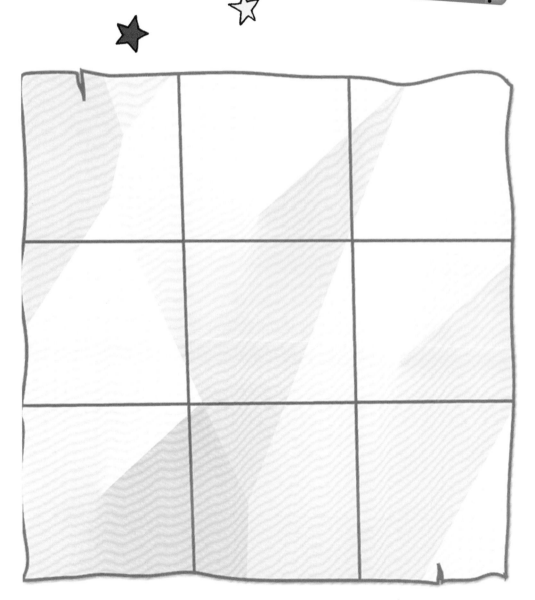

1. Glue the two centre squares together. When dried, open out one of the sheets, place a silver coin in the centre and fold the paper, following the lines on the template, so that it covers the coin. Turn the wallet over and open out the other sheet. You are now ready to perform the trick.

①

2. Show your audience the sheet of paper and place the copper coin in the centre. Fold the paper over the coin.

②

3. On the very last fold, turn the whole packet over. Wave your hands over the packet and then open it to reveal the silver coin in place of the bronze coin. Your audience will be amazed!

③

Five to One

This trick is very easy to do and looks really impressive!

1. Ask a volunteer to place a coin in each hand. Make sure that you cannot see which coin goes in which hand – you could turn your back.

①

2. Tell the volunteer to multiply the value of the coin in their left hand by two. Tell them not to say the number, but keep it in their mind. If they don't say 'yes', ask them almost straight away if they have the answer. Notice how long they take to answer.

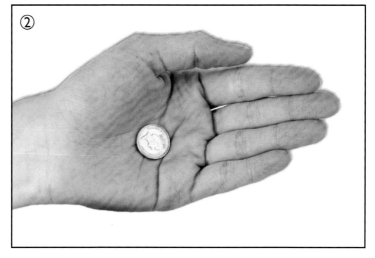

②

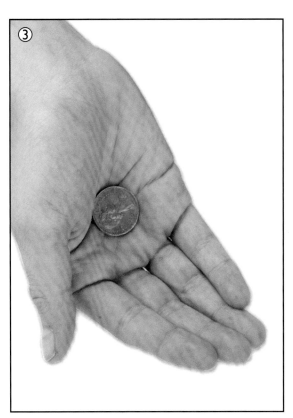

③

3. Now ask them to multiply the coin in their right hand by seventeen. Notice how long it takes this time. From the pauses for thinking of the answers, you can work out which coin is in which hand.

But How?

If the 5p is in the left hand, you will know this because both pauses for the calculation will be very short (two times five, and one times seventeen).

If the 5p is in the right hand, you will know this because it takes a longer time to multiply five by seventeen. If the penny was in the right hand, then the pause would be short because the calculation one times seventeen is easy.

Find the Lady

Four ordinary cards and a queen are placed in envelopes. Even though the envelopes are mixed up, you can tell which one contains the queen.

Props box

- Five identical empty envelopes
- Five playing cards (one has to be a queen)
- A coin

1. Show five empty envelopes and five playing cards, one of which is a queen. Ask a volunteer to hand you an envelope and one of the cards.

2. Place the card in the envelope and drop the envelope on the table. Do exactly the same with the other envelopes and cards.

3. What the volunteer does not know is the cards are placed in the envelopes horizontally (on their sides) but when the queen is placed in an envelope, it is secretly turned as soon as it is out of sight so it stands vertically (upright).

④

4. Mix the envelopes and hold them behind your back. Feel each envelope and find which one holds the queen. Because it is positioned differently from the other cards, it is easy to find.

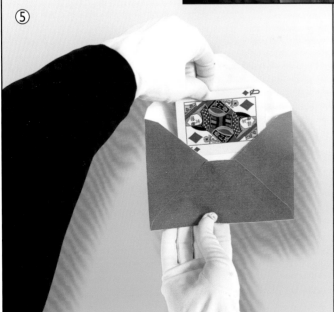

⑤

5. Bring the queen envelope forward, reach into it and turn the queen to a horizontal position before taking it out of the envelope.

Do as I Do

You and a volunteer each choose a card – and by a magical coincidence you both pick the same one!

Props box

• Two packs of cards

1. You will need two packs of cards. The volunteer takes one pack and you have the other.

2. Ask the volunteer to do exactly the same as you. Give your pack a shuffle and ask the volunteer to do the same.

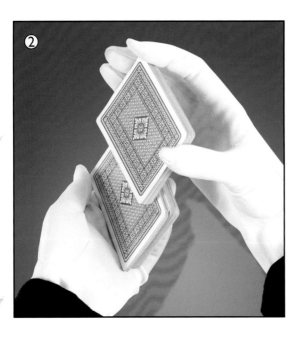
②

3. You now exchange packs – but when handing your pack to the volunteer, you take a secret glimpse at the bottom card. Remember that card.

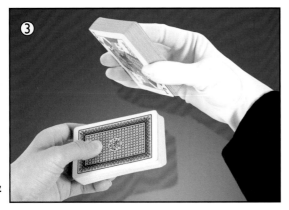
③

4. From the pack that you now hold take out one card, look at it and put it on top of the pack. As the volunteer does the same, say, 'Remember your card.' You do not have to remember the card you take.

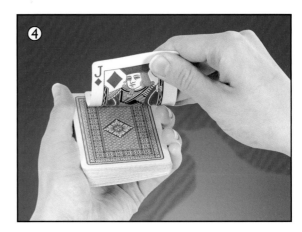
④

5. You both now cut the pack so the chosen card is lost somewhere in the middle.

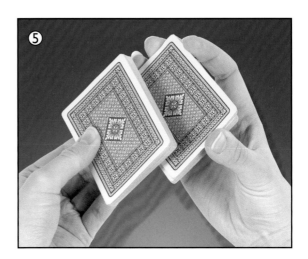
⑤

6. Exchange packs once again. Ask the volunteer to go through the pack, remove the chosen card, and place it face down on the table.

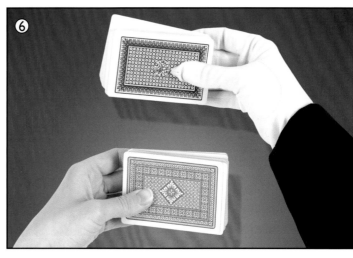

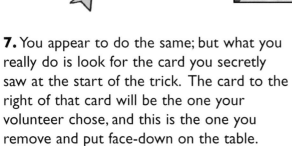

7. You appear to do the same; but what you really do is look for the card you secretly saw at the start of the trick. The card to the right of that card will be the one your volunteer chose, and this is the one you remove and put face-down on the table.

8. Both cards are now turned over, and everyone is amazed to see that they are the same!

Shrinking Coins

Make coins shrink and grow simply by touching them!

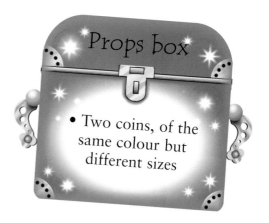

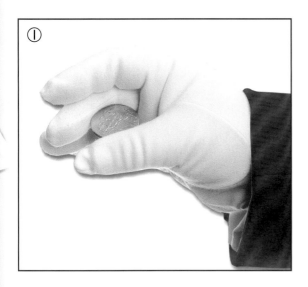

Props box

- Two coins, of the same colour but different sizes

1. Start by holding the larger coin horizontally between your second finger and thumb.

②

2. Hold the smaller coin upright between your finger and thumb. Move your hand backwards and forwards so that your hand can be seen, but not the larger coin.

3. Now bring your other hand across and take the coins in the same grip, but this time swap the coins so that the smaller one is horizontal and the larger one is upright.

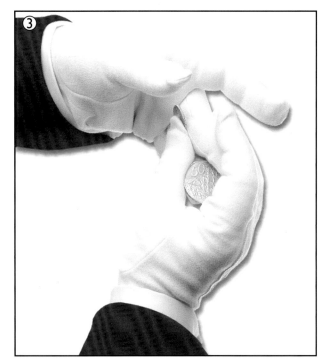

4. Your audience will think that the upright coin has grown!

5. If you now reverse step 3, the coin will appear to shrink again.

Money Maker

If you prepare this trick properly, it will baffle your audience. It is very simple to perform.

Props box

- Empty matchbox, any size will do
- Coin
- Magic wand

Preparation

Hide a coin between the drawer and the sleeve of a matchbox, as shown in the picture left.

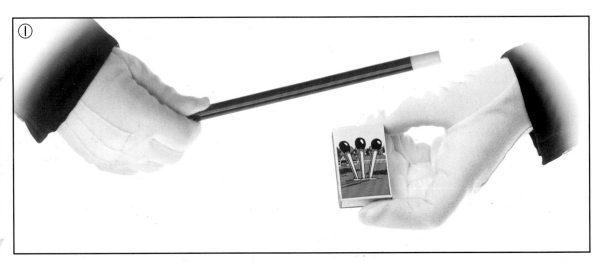

①

1. Produce your matchbox and open it halfway, so that the hidden coin cannot be seen. Ask a volunteer to lend you two coins and drop these into the box. Close the drawer, and explain that with just a wave of your magic wand, the magic box will make the money increase.

②

2. Give the box a shake and say a few magic words. When you open the box, you will reveal three coins instead of two! You'll be very popular!